What Makes a Great Training Organization?

A Handbook of Best Practices

Doug Harward
Ken Taylor

Vice President, Publisher: Tim Moore
Associate Publisher and Director of Marketing: Amy Neidlinger
Development Editor: Russ Hall
Operations Specialist: Jodi Kemper
Cover Designer: Chuti Prasertsith
Managing Editor: Kristy Hart
Project Editor: Andy Beaster
Copy Editor: Kitty Wilson
Proofreader: Katie Matejka
Indexer: Tim Wright
Compositor: Nonie Ratcliff
Manufacturing Buyer: Dan Uhrig

Pearson offers excellent discounts on this book when ordered in quantity for bulk purchases or special sales. For more information, please contact U.S. Corporate and Government Sales, 1-800-382-3419, corpsales@pearsontechgroup.com. For sales outside the U.S., please contact International Sales at international@pearsoned.com.

First Printing March 2014

ISBN-10: 0-13-349196-X
ISBN-13: 978-0-13-349196-8

Pearson Education LTD.
Pearson Education Australia PTY, Limited
Pearson Education Singapore, Pte. Ltd.
Pearson Education Asia, Ltd.
Pearson Education Canada, Ltd.
Pearson Educación de Mexico, S.A. de C.V.
Pearson Education—Japan
Pearson Education Malaysia, Pte. Ltd.

Library of Congress Control Number: 2013957861

This book is dedicated to all of those training profes-
sionals who work tirelessly to make sure they provide
the type of training and development programs that
truly impact the lives of the learners, while ultimately
transforming the performance of their business.

Contents

Acknowledgments

We would like to thank our wives and children for their unending and unwavering support. Kim (Doug) and Cheri, Samantha and Christopher (Ken) have supported us unconditionally in our career endeavors and been there for us when we worked late, traveled to be with clients, or sat on the sofa with a laptop reviewing research information and client data. In addition, we would like to thank our staff at Training Industry, Inc. for their commitment to our profession, this project, and our many clients.

About the Authors

Doug Harward is the CEO and Founder of Training Industry, Inc. He is internationally recognized as one of the leading strategists for training and outsourcing business models. He is respected as one of the industry's leading authorities on competitive analysis for training services and works with international companies and new business start-ups in building training organizations. Harward previously served as the Director of Global Learning for Nortel Networks. He received the Chairman's Global Award for Community Service for his work in developing integrated learning organization strategies within higher education, public schools and business. He has worked in the training industry for more than 25 years. He received an MBA from the Fuqua School of Business at Duke University and a BSBA in Marketing from Appalachian State University.

Ken Taylor is Partner and Chief Operating Officer of Training Industry, Inc., and editor in chief for *Training Industry Magazine*. His career spans over 25 years in leadership and entrepreneur roles across several industries and focus areas, including operations, technology, sales and marketing, and finance, including serving as CFO of several large business units. Taylor's expertise and experience includes organization design and development, corporate learning and development, marketing strategy (B2B and B2C), research, enterprise technologies, product marketing and sales management, strategic planning and strategic acquisition management. He holds a bachelor's degree from McGill University in Finance and International Business.

Introduction: Why We Wrote This Book

In 2007, we sought to understand the criteria organizations used when doling out awards to training organizations for the work they do. We found out there was little depth to the criteria, and there wasn't any deep understanding of what practices are actually important in making a training organization exceptional, or *great* (an important distinction). We sought a better understanding. So we did our first study of what capabilities and practices training organizations employ in order to perform at a very high level.

What we found is that there are groups of processes, or practices, that when done well, drive sustainable impact and make a significant difference in the performance of a business. We call these groups of practices *capabilities*. Our research showed that virtually all training organizations have some level of expertise in eight capability areas. Training organizations that excel in some of these capability areas are considered to be high performing. And those that excel in many of the practices among the eight capability areas are considered to be performing at what we consider a *great* level.

Some companies, such as suppliers, monetize these capabilities. Others employ them in running training for their own constituents. We sought to understand and codify the "best practices" associated with each capability area. We spent several years on this, revising our data each year, and we believe we now have a very good understanding of what the best practices are around the core capability areas for running a training organization. Then we had the idea of writing this book to educate individuals about what the practices are and to show how training managers can use these practices in their everyday work life.

We were often asked a seemingly simple question in our discussions with learning leaders: "I know we have to make some changes, but where should we start?" The need for this book became more real as we started to understand that there was no blueprint or roadmap to help leaders understand what the collective body of corporate learning experts—and those actually doing the role—felt were the activities or practices required to make an organization great at supporting learning. As business-focused professionals, our goal was to shorten the learning curve, to tap the collective wisdom to help the next generation of learning leaders skip some of the trial and error, and go right to implementation of practices that will change the impact of their organization. We felt that we needed to both rank the impact or importance of the practices of great training organizations and also group these practices around the known processes found in almost all corporate training environments.

In our research, we were able to look at the market from several perspectives, including job roles/constituents, companies of all sizes, and companies from multiple industry segments. Our study represents all of the market.

The Demographics of the Research Pool

Our report included the opinions of 1,609 learning professionals, collected through online surveys. A 2008 study elicited 462 respondents, and a 2009 study elicited 364. In 2010, 183 learning leaders contributed to the study, and an additional 221 and 192 took part in 2011 and 2012, respectively. Finally, in 2013, 187 learning leaders responded to the survey. Throughout the entire cycle, we continuously validated the results through hundreds of discussions with both the supply-side companies and corporate learning leaders throughout the industry.

Respondents were learning professionals who represent or run three basic types of organizations:

- **Corporate training departments**—These organizations train those who work for, or with, their own organizations (e.g., employees, channel partners, contractors) or customers of their organizations' non-training-related products. They may also buy training products or services from training companies or providers.

- **Training companies/providers**—These organizations train external client organizations (e.g., corporate training departments) or individuals to whom they sell training-related products or services, which may also include consulting. This group also includes some nonprofits, and other organizations, such as membership and trade associations, which offer training to external parties.

- **Educational institutions**—This group includes universities or colleges that provide education to their students and others who cannot be classified into the two main categories above.

The sizes of the organizations represented in our study are displayed in Figure I-1. The varied sizes of the organizations demonstrate that the best practices addressed in the book represent all of the industry, not just big companies.

While training and development, technology, and banking/finance were the top 3 industries represented, respondents from corporate training departments spanned more than 20 industries, as shown in Figure I-2.

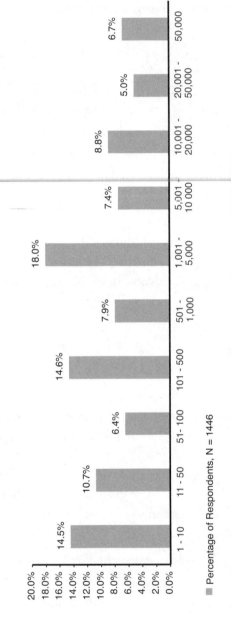

■ Percentage of Respondents, N = 1446

Figure I-1 Sizes of Companies, Represented by Number of Employees, 2008–2013

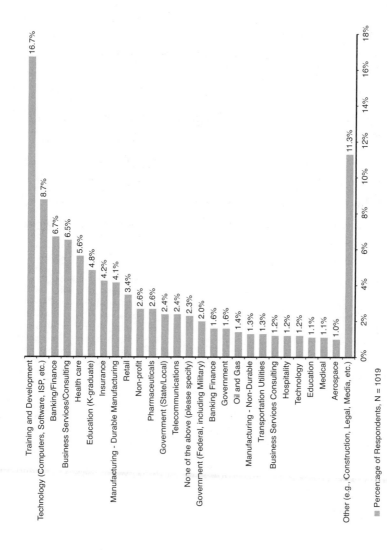

Training and Development 16.7%
Technology (Computers, Software, ISP, etc.) 8.7%
Banking/Finance 6.7%
Business Services/Consulting 6.5%
Health care 5.6%
Education (K-graduate) 4.8%
Insurance 4.2%
Manufacturing - Durable Manufacturing 4.1%
Retail 3.4%
Non-profit 2.6%
Pharmaceuticals 2.6%
Government (State/Local) 2.4%
Telecommunications 2.4%
None of the above (please specify) 2.3%
Government (Federal, including Military) 2.0%
Banking Finance 1.6%
Government 1.6%
Oil and Gas 1.4%
Manufacturing - Non-Durable 1.3%
Transportation Utilities 1.3%
Business Services Consulting 1.2%
Hospitality 1.2%
Technology 1.2%
Education 1.1%
Medical 1.1%
Aerospace 1.0%
Other (e.g., Construction, Legal, Media, etc.) 11.3%

0% 2% 4% 6% 8% 10% 12% 14% 16% 18%

▨ Percentage of Respondents, N = 1019

Figure I-2 Industries Represented, 2009–2013

This book explores the capabilities and best practices associated with each capability, as defined by our report. We frequently informally mention people who provided input throughout the research; to protect their privacy, we do not name them or their companies. Where we can, however, we do provide their names and companies. All the data and information presented in this book come from real companies doing real training. The goal of this book is to provide you with some ideas—a starting point to help you transform your organization—that we feel play critical roles in the long-term success of any company. Remember that as the custodian of the significant investment your company makes in the development of its people, you are responsible for maximizing the impact of that investment. The following chapters offer a set of practical strategies, tools, and practices that can help you with that challenge. We spend almost every day at the heart of the training industry. We look forward to your feedback, as we will continue to track, adjust, and share our understanding of what makes a great training organization.

1

The Eight Process Capability Areas of a Training Organization

Leaders of high-performing training organizations understand that achieving the level of excellence that their clients expect requires a strong commitment to process. Our research tells us that focus on process is not enough on its own; success depends on demonstration of process—or an organization's ability to perform that process at a high level. When we began our research, the fundamental question we wanted to answer was, "What practices are associated with the capabilities that, when performed at a very high level, make a training organization *great*?"

We surveyed learning leaders from a variety of industries all over the world to determine which process capabilities are the most important. While contributing their valuable opinions to identify the most critical process capabilities, these leaders also told us the practices that propel training organizations through the transformation from *good* to *great*. Learning leaders then rated how well their own training organizations perform each process capability to confirm which processes are truly *critical* and to pinpoint potential areas for improvement.

The Eight Key Process Capabilities

When we asked learning leaders to rate which process capabilities were important in a great training organization, eight capabilities emerged as being most critical. We developed the cited practices through discussion with the research participants and other learning leaders into the following eight key process capabilities areas:

- **Strategic alignment**—Ability to design learning programs that align with business objectives.
- **Content development**—Assessment, design, management, and maintenance of content.
- **Delivery**—Ability to manage an instructor network and deliver training using multiple modalities.
- **Diagnostics**—Ability to identify causes of problems and make recommendations.
- **Reporting and analysis**—Ability to define business metrics and report data to make improvements.
- **Technology integration**—Ability to integrate learning technologies with other learning technologies or other corporate applications.
- **Administrative services**—Ability to manage scheduling, registration, technology, and other back office support functions.
- **Portfolio management**—Ability to manage, rationalize, and maintain large portfolios of learning solutions.

The greatest number of respondents (79%) rated strategic alignment as critical, and the second largest number of respondents (55%) said content development is critical. Figure 1-1 shows the percentage of respondents who rated each process capability as critical for great training organizations.

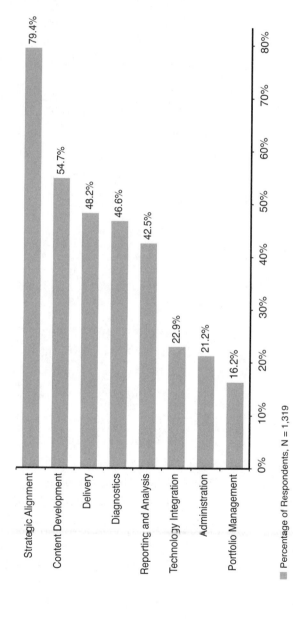

Percentage of Respondents, N = 1,319

Figure 1-1 Percentage of Respondents Rating Each Process Capability as Critical for a Great Training Organization

Although Figure 1-1 demonstrates the need for great training organizations to possess many of the process capabilities listed, some capabilities are clearly considered more critical than others. When we asked learning leaders to specify which process capability is most critical for a great training organization, an overwhelming 59% reiterated the importance of strategic alignment, as shown in Figure 1-2.

Learning leaders provided us with a very clear picture of where to start in improving the impact of a training organization. The old adage "if the program isn't aligned with the goals of the business, then it's probably not going to generate the type of impact it should" rings clear in the results of the survey.

We explore each of these process capabilities further in other chapters.

Organization Ratings

We asked learning leaders to rate their own training organizations' proficiency for each process capability area, using the scale "don't do," "poor," "average," "good," and "great." Figure 1-3 shows the percentage of respondents who rated their own training organization as great for each process capability.

We found it interesting that learning leaders reported that their own training organizations excelled at the three most critical process capabilities, as outlined in Figure 1-2: strategic alignment, content development, and delivery. In addition, few learning leaders (no more than 27.5%) rated their organizations as great in any of the process capability areas. This information leads us to believe that there are a large number of organizations ready for ideas to help them move their organization along toward greatness.

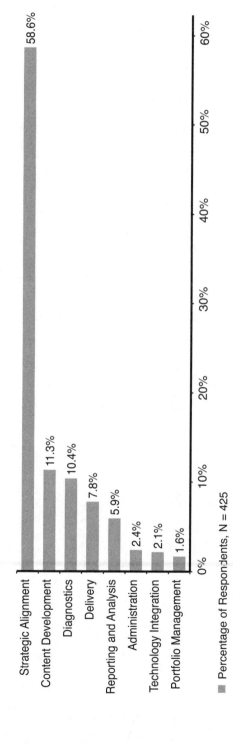

Figure 1-2   The Most Critical Process Capabilities for a Great Training Organization

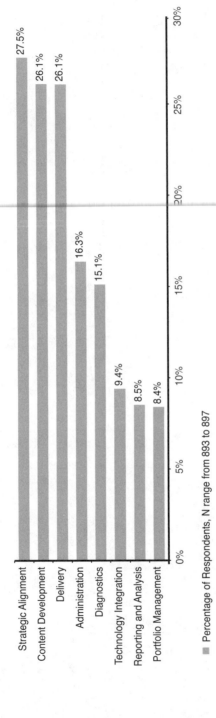

- Percentage of Respondents, N range from 893 to 897

Figure 1-3 Respondents Rating Their Training Organization as Great for Each Process Capability

Understanding process capabilities is the first and most integral step in determining what is important to continually improving the operations of a training organization. Many articles, books, and other available materials suggest innovative ideas for how to run a training organization. Some suggest that you run your organization like a business. Others suggest that you should evolve from an academic approach to a business approach to training. All surely have merit and are important to consider when determining what is important in running a high-performing training organization. But we believe the research suggests that the best path is to fundamentally understand the process capabilities that are critical in great training organizations and then work to implement those practices that have been identified by hundreds of training leaders around the globe.

We suggest that you determine where your organization is related to each practice within the various capability areas and define priorities for the practices that are most important to your organization, based on corporate goals and objectives. Although hundreds of professionals told us their opinions and helped us identify the priorities for a large number of organizations, what is more important is that you determine what is important for *your* organization. After you do that, you can develop a plan for how to make your organization a great, high-performing training organization.

Please recognize that the process capabilities and practices are *not* mutually exclusive. That is, you can implement any and all of them at the same time, or at various times, depending on your business's objectives. It's up to you. What works for one organization may not be best in another. You are the best judge of what your strategy should be. We just suggest that you take a path and begin your journey to becoming a great training organization.

Conclusion

The chapters that follow explore the process capabilities and practices that define a great training organization. Strategic alignment, which aligns training programs with the business needs and goals of a company, is consistently considered the most crucial process capability for training organizations to master. By using the best practices that learning leaders identified to excel at strategic alignment, as well as the best practices for the other process capabilities, a training organization can improve performance and become a *great training organization that contributes value to the business.*

2

The Importance of Learning Leadership

A leader in a training organization can be a VP to whom hundreds of people report, or a person in a midsize company responsible for a team of 10 to 20 people, or even an individual running training for a small company. Regardless of the organization or the type of training leader, anyone who manages training should aim for greatness. The important factors in making a training organization great are how various practices contribute to making the company great—or at least helping the organization perform at a higher level—and how the leader of the organization impacts the business by employing those practices in the organization's daily processes.

Numerous ideas have been published on what training organizations should do to be more effective, especially in regard to creating better training. Our focus here is not on how to create better courses or training events but on what you as a training leader can do to help your organization perform at the highest level. We focus on the very specific practices or processes that have been found to be the most important practices to employ. Sure, there are many more ideas and practices we can conjure up other than the ones listed in this book, but the idea is to define the specific practices that you can focus on with the limited time, energy, and resources you have so you and your organization can get the most impact for your investment.

Of course, creating a great training organization is essential in creating a great company. For any company that is recognized in the market for being great, you can be sure that the training organization inside that company contributed to that success. In what many consider to be one of the best business books of all time, *In Search of Excellence*, Tom Peters and Robert Waterman say that companies that are great have a common trait: They are focused on organizational effectiveness.

The way to organizational effectiveness is through your people. Virtually every one of the companies mentioned in *In Search of Excellence* has a strong focus on developing people. It is easy to recognize a good organization, whether large or small. Good organizations are survivors and can adapt to change. They manage resources and run at peak performance. They are in tune with their capabilities, and everyone is on board with the company's mission and the objectives that take the company where it needs to go. And the organization's training is aligned to the needs of the business.

The first and most important responsibility of a training leader is to make sure that the training in the organization is aligned to the needs of the company. Here we introduce you to what we believe is the new order of training management. It is a paradigm shift, an evolution from an academically oriented corporate university made up of many training courses based on what employees like or dislike (or what they believe is important in helping them to develop their career) to a lean organization focused on mission-critical training that has a direct impact on the overall performance of the business. Ultimately, the shift involves the individuals within the business because they are the ones who make the organization successful.

When a large pharmaceutical company spends hundreds of millions of dollars on developing a new product, the success of that product being adopted by the market is not left to chance. It is achieved through a very thorough and orchestrated approach to training the sales force and detailing the product information to the influencers in the market (doctors, pharmacists, and insurance companies). The pharmaceutical company's mission is to make sure all the people in the supply chain have the right information and that the product is brought to market in the fastest and most efficient manner. It's about speed to market, getting the product adopted and delivered fast, and ultimately generating as much revenue as possible to repay the huge investment required to create the product. The company leaves little to chance.

We believe that great organizations are led by great training leaders who view their role as vital to the success of their companies. They schedule regular meetings with the senior management of the organization to get the real picture of the critical objectives of the organization. They bring to the table ideas and strategies that demonstrate how training can ultimately move the needle on those objectives. In a word, they leverage the time they get with senior management or their shot at having a seat at the table to demonstrate their understanding of the company's objectives. They are objective and goal junkies who are always looking to find new and innovative ways to enable success inside the organization.

We have noticed that great training leaders preach alignment, focus, interdependence, and efficiency in the solutions they recommend. That tone affords them a place in the discussion, and their deep understanding of the dynamics impacting the company's ability to meet their objectives allows them to bring a unique consultative viewpoint to the senior team in the company. They are students of the corporation's objectives and goals. They are always looking for changes in the goals to ensure that they are developing relevant programs to help the company's people gain the skill set necessary to execute on the objectives. They also focus on rooting out investment in noncritical activities and redirecting that investment into the right training for employees on the skills they need for driving the mission-critical objectives. They earn their position at the table by contributing to the company's success—just like the head of research, product development, or manufacturing does.

Conclusion

Success in training comes from leadership—not from courses or programs. *Successful training courses come from successful leadership practices.* Training leaders own the responsibility of deciding what training is needed, in partnership with their clients, based on the clients' needs. Training leaders can, and should, have a huge impact on the success of a business, in addition to the success of a training organization.

When a training organization is not viewed as strategic, or when it is viewed as not contributing what is needed for the success of the organizational goals of the business, training leaders must determine what they can do differently. Strategic alignment ensures that training leaders understand what must be done differently and what must continue to be done at a high level. Chapter 3 defines how to determine what training is needed and vital to survival—not just nice to have.

3

Strategic Alignment

The single most important factor that impacts whether a training organization is viewed as an integral part of the business or as being great is whether it is strategically aligned to what the business needs. In essence, strategic alignment is an organization's ability to design learning interventions, programs, and processes for training in a way that supports the specific mission-critical objectives of the organization or objectives on behalf of what the individual clients need. Strategic alignment involves beginning with the end in mind—determining the performance expectations of the training and then designing and delivering training to meet those specific objectives.

The way a pharmaceutical company goes about its business tells a wonderful story of how the business has very specific objectives and how the training of the sales force is designed to help achieve that objective. The company's measure of success may be speed to market, which equates to revenues within the first quarter of launch.

Or consider a licensed practical nurse (LPN) who has been working in an oncology ward but is showing signs of stress because of the nature of the patients and the high incidence of loss of life. For her own good, the LPN is being switched over to pediatrics, in a transfer approved by the hospital's chief of staff. The LPN's day-to-day job responsibilities will still be to provide care and support to patients (as well as to ensure their safety and prevent risk). But the needs of young children are different from those of the majority of patients the

LPN has worked with in oncology. The doctors with whom she will work in this ward have specialty training, and the LPN must also have mission-critical training to focus on quite different aspects of caring for the safety and well-being of those in the pediatrics ward.

There are many examples of how organizations align training to the needs of their business, and we're sure you can see many right within your own business. But to understand strategic alignment, we think it's important to delve into the real reasons corporate executives invest the many dollars they do on training. Some believe employee training is done to create a more satisfied employee or customer; or maybe it is done to improve the performance of the workforce or to ensure that customers know how to use a product. While these reasons actually do exist, they are in some ways benefits attained from training, not the fundamental reasons dollars are invested.

Understanding the strategic reasons companies provide training is very important to understanding strategic alignment. Being able to answer the question "Is this training strategically aligned to the needs of the business?" or "Is it a nice thing to have?" can help management differentiate which programs have value and which of them waste valuable resources. If, as a manager, you can answer the question of how training is strategically aligned to the business, then you can feel comfortable knowing you are spending the company's money wisely. We believe when you do this type of rationalization exercise, you should consider the following three reasons companies invest dollars in training. And if you can relate your reason to train to one of these three, it generally will pass the litmus test for alignment:

- **Reduce costs** (e.g., improve efficiency, reduce turnover, reduce the cost of failure)—The first and most often considered reason for training is to improve the performance of the individuals inside the organization. But the primary reason organizations provide training is to ultimately reduce the cost of operations or services. For example, when a company provides training to manufacturing employees, the objective is to get them to perform at a level that increases their capacity to increase production or to minimize mistakes. Each of these has a direct impact on costs. If you can improve the efficiency of a line worker, you can produce more goods, thus reducing the unit cost of each good produced. This goes back to the days of Frederick Taylor, the father of scientific management. His early work, which was instrumental to companies like U.S. Steel and Ford, focused on how jobs were engineered to keep the cost of labor at a minimum. His philosophy holds true today: If you train your employees to do the job "right," with fewer mistakes, you can reduce the costs of failure, and you can reduce the costs associated with doing things that do not add value to the business.

- **Generate revenue** (e.g., improve sales, retain customers, improve service quality)—Almost every company that has some degree of technological orientation in its products or services is expected—or even required—to train customers on how to install, use, or maintain its products or services. This training can be sold directly to the customer as an add-on service, or it can sometimes be included as part of the initial sale. Consider Caterpillar, which sells earth-moving equipment. Caterpillar's customers assume the responsibility to maintain and utilize the equipment. A customer's staff has to be trained on how to use and support and maintain the equipment. The cost of doing that training is built into the price of the equipment and is passed on to the customer.

- **Mitigate risks**—The third and often least understood reason training is provided is to mitigate, or at least minimize, the risks associated with the improper use or consumption of a product. Again consider Caterpillar. If a customer's staff is not trained on how to use the equipment properly and people are subsequently injured because they did not know how to use certain safety features, the liability associated with that mistake could be the responsibility of Caterpillar. As another example, consider the responsibility of a hospital to make sure all staff are properly trained to do their jobs correctly.

Our research has found that training professionals continue to emphasize the indisputable position of strategic alignment as the most essential attribute or capability of great training organizations. Without it, they say, training can be pointless, ineffective, and disappointing. A company that has a mission to grow but doesn't prepare its employees for how to grow the business is going to have a hard time fulfilling its mission. One leadership development coordinator put it this way: "There is little point to training if it doesn't tie in to the core mission of the organization. Fail in this area, and it won't be long until you're polishing up your resume."

A training program supervisor told us, "A strong alignment with business objectives helps focus learning programs on must-have issues, topics, and success criteria—which increases the training's value to the organization and justifies the drain on resources—both staffing and financial."

We have found that employees want to understand how their performance impacts the business, and by aligning training and business goals, they can actually see—and deliver—quantifiable results. Hospitals post (and promote) their safety records and ability to minimalize risk, with the goal of making future patients feel safer while boosting the pride and morale of the staff. As a training organization develops a unified effort to understand and meet the needs of clients and the organization, it becomes a trusted advisor. It generates buy-in and executive support for training that may be subsequently proposed.

Sales employees at Nordstrom stores have long been empowered to act wisely on behalf of the company—to go the extra mile to ensure that customers have the ultimate experience. While accepting a return or helping a customer find the right department is not directly tied to an individual's sales bonus, each salesperson realizes that anything that is good for the company and its overriding success will benefit everyone in the organization. This knowledge doesn't come to employees by chance. It is taught to sales employees early, and it is expected of them in their day-to-day activities. At the same time, this knowledge empowers them.

Focusing on business needs and validating business results keeps training organizations accountable for performance. When held to the same standards as other business units, training organizations are expected to constantly evaluate how their programs will drive business value—whether by improving job performance, increasing employee engagement, or reducing turnover.

Strategic alignment requires more than aligning with an organization's current business needs. It also involves anticipating an organization's future needs—even if they are years off. A common strategy of forward-thinking companies is to hire entry-level employees directly out of college, provide them with training about the company and its industry, and teach them the foundational leadership skills that will carry them for years to come. New hires in companies like these are not hired based on their experience and accomplishments in their professional life but based on their potential to be great leaders in the future. This approach is exemplified by Milliken and Company, headquartered in Spartanburg, South Carolina, and ranked as one of the world's top 20 training organizations by London's *Financial Times*. Milliken has a rigorous and comprehensive management orientation program that is designed to provide employees with the skills they need in their first role, as well as the knowledge to continue their development that will carry them into many roles in management over the succeeding years.

Strategic Alignment Practices

When done correctly, strategic alignment of training initiatives resembles in many ways the exercise many companies undertake when performing organizational alignment companywide. We strongly believe that the tactics and practices developed to support organizational alignment should be used to ensure that a company's training initiatives are aligned with the company's critical objectives. You can choose your model of choice, but the end result is to ensure that the activities of your training organization align with the goals of the company, and we have identified several practices that can help with this challenge. The following sections detail the five most important strategic alignment practices found in great training organizations.

In our research, at least 89% of the respondents considered five practices related to strategic alignment to be critical (see Figure 3-1). The following sections explain these practices.

Develop Consultative Partnerships with Clients

To ensure that training is properly aligned to the needs of a business, a training leader must be in direct communication with those who set the strategy of the company. This communication helps the training leader understand the direction and needs of the business. Through this communication, the leader is able to implement solutions that ensure that training meets the needs of the business. Working in tandem with the corporate executives of the business requires a training leader to take a consultative approach to understanding requirements and identifying and designing solutions based on the client's needs. As a part of the research, one organizational development manager told us not to think of training organizations as ones that just deliver courses. Rather, he said, we should think about the role of the organization in this way: "By aligning your training programs with business objectives, your training organization becomes a business partner—a team that all levels of the organization can trust, rely on, and one that is critical to the continued success of the business."

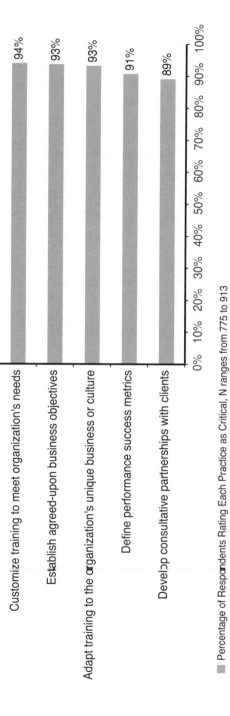

Percentage of Respondents Rating Each Practice as Critical, N ranges from 775 to 913

Figure 3-1 Critical Strategic Alignment Practices

As one global education manager of a consumer product distribution company said, "We deeply collaborate with the client as an extension of their team." Such teamwork and partnerships—where there is a healthy and equal interchange between the clients and their training partners—are more likely to result in true strategic alignment and to have better training and business outcomes.

In one such partnership, a learning supervisor in an email marketing firm confirms that training partners are included in customers' monthly business reviews, during which they gain valuable insight into training opportunities. In describing his company's training organization, a director of training says, "Everything we design, develop, and deliver ties directly into our strategic business initiatives. This is so critical to our company that the training organization reports directly into the office of strategy management."

Establish Agreed-Upon Business Objectives

At the most basic level, training organizations and their clients must come to an agreement about *why* they are providing training and what expectations each have about the training they are providing. This requires training leaders to ask the right questions as well as to listen and interpret the needs of each client. They must put aside sales-level discussions of their training programs until they have established the client's training needs.

While having a client focus is essential for establishing agreed-upon objectives, more effort is required to ensure that training objectives meet real business needs. Rather than accept clients' stated requirements and requests for training, strategic alignment forces training organizations to dig deeper and take a closer look at genuine training needs. You must ask what problem or business opportunity training should address, how it is identified, and how it will impact the organization's success.

For example, when a seasonal toys manufacturer is implementing a new strategic sales initiative, the training organization should be involved early in the planning process. Acting as a consultant to the sales executive, the training leader should seek the best way to measure how well the training performs the sales organization's objectives—in this case, the critical mission of sales made at certain times of the year for the products to be on hand at another time of the year. This not only ensures that goals and success metrics are clearly identified, but it also provides consistency across departments and throughout the company.

Establishing agreed-upon objectives entails the following:

- Defining the sales strategy and training goals and creating metrics to measure effectiveness.

- Agreeing on the roles, responsibilities, and actions of sales leadership to support the change effort.

- Facilitating group planning sessions to ensure that the linkage between the strategic initiative and the training activity is understood.

A director of training and development at a Fortune 500 company told us, "When all parties are **not** involved in the strategic planning phase, leaders begin to rely on training as a break–fix mechanism, not as a learning or business solution." The leader of a major pharmaceutical company's corporate university said, "You need a clear vision for how learning can impact the business and get results."

How do training organizations link training to business objectives? One of the best ways is by an activity mentioned by a corporate training leader in a health care company, who said that every one of the company's courses has a written objective that ties to a business need. Consider some of the needs a health care company might have: risk management, safety, top-shelf cleanliness, and a general bedside manner in all employees (from doctors to nurses to housekeepers) that is both efficient and caring. When these needs are written into objectives and included as part of training, they feed the desired culture and align *everyone* to the experience each patient will have.

Define Performance Success Metrics

The primary role of great training organizations is to improve the performance of the business. Once clients and a training organization establish agreed-upon objectives, verifiable results or success metrics for the specific training initiative can be established. By defining which metrics need to shift, and by how much, for the training to be considered successful, a training organization gets a clear measure of the true alignment of learning programs.

A vice president for education services at a software company put it this way: "Training organizations need defined performance success metrics—not just training metrics, but business transformation metrics as well. This will show the success and value of training programs." A performance success metric measures the quantifiable results of training, both for senior management and for those who were trained.

The right combination of metrics can show where the company is succeeding and by how much, and it can also put the spotlight on areas of weakness. Such metrics can identify trends and places where management can take steps to improve performance. For example, a one-year training program to boost the performance of sales staff may demonstrate 6% growth in sales, which would more than offset the cost of training. From that result, the strategic planning team could develop additional specific execution targets. If the expected results do not materialize, and there are no offsetting economic conditions or other reasons for the shortfall, then the training processes themselves may need to be scrutinized.

Customize Training to Meet the Organization's Needs

When training organizations truly listen and understand the needs of those they serve, off-the-shelf programs may not fit the bill. Training professionals may have to tailor standard programs, or even create new ones, to align the material with the specific needs of the business. Consider the training that NASA provides to astronauts. All astronauts are expected to complete basic training, which provides the general skills they need for virtually any endeavor. But they also need training related to the missions they are assigned to, and that training is designed specifically for each mission. No two mission training programs are the same; rather, the training is specific to the tasks associated with each mission.

A number of drivers influence when training should be customized to the learner or learners:

- **Learners' skill levels**—Training activities may need to be adapted to the varying skill levels of learners.
- **Job tasks**—It may be important to incorporate specific tasks associated with the short-term mission of the job.
- **Culture**—Training must often incorporate cultural nuances, such as societal behaviors, ethnicity, or religious differences.
- **Geography**—Training must sometimes incorporate considerations related to where the learner is located.
- **Language**—Training content must often be customized for various languages, most often from English to French, Mandarin, Spanish, etc.
- **Localization**—Training content and delivery should sometimes be customized based on local norms, such as processes or practices within a local facility.

- **Industry specific**—Training content and delivery should sometimes be customized based on differences between industries, such as sales training for pharmaceutical firms versus sales training for heavy machinery companies.

Whatever training you use will be most relevant if it is tailored to fit exactly right. A performance management and training leader at an architectural and general contracting firm stressed the need for customization: "I have found that training that is not easily customizable to our organization is a waste of our time and resources."

When leaders discuss what they value in organizations that offer customized training, they mention *flexibility* and *adaptability* most frequently. Even if a training program is initially aligned with business goals, over time it may need to be realigned and re-customized to continuously meet the organization's evolving needs. If the business target has changed, the training must also change.

A training analyst in a state health insurance company said that his organization has "created a framework to map courses and programs to specific business processes and roles." This allows the organization to understand the level of customization needed. There's nothing wrong with mapping out an overview that encompasses a company's aims, its needs, and how it intends to get its people—new or entrenched—in line with that overview.

Adapt Training to the Organization's Unique Business or Culture

All learners are different, and all learners learn differently. *Adapting training* refers to modifying the delivery of existing content to better meet the needs of the learner or business. Adapting training differs from customizing training; whereas *customizing* refers to modifying content, *adapting* refers to modifying the delivery of the content.

Examples of adaptation strategies you should consider include modality (elearning versus asynchronous or synchronous virtual instruction), the time of day the class is delivered, the type of facilities used for training (classroom or labs), the technology platforms used to deliver content, and more.

Many organizations in our research emphasized the importance of investing time and resources into learning a client's line of business so they could effectively adapt the training to how the client wanted to receive it. For example, one finance training manager spent time getting to know the needs of an organization by setting up a series of regular "needs" discussions with the senior finance team, first to understand the changes in their objectives and then to get the leadership perspective on the shifting development need of the employees in the department and how to best deliver the training. This helped the finance training manager ensure that he understood the context in which the major move to virtual instructor-led training and webinars could work in support of the compliance training for the company's accountants.

Training organizations must also consider what types of learning solutions both support company goals and integrate well with the organization's culture. For instance, in a sales-driven company, training may be an interactive experience, incorporating the sales mantra through instructor-led training and coaching and incorporating sales techniques through role-play simulations or serious games. Reinforcing the company's culture and processes through a range of training methods will help employees become more engaged and more productive—and that will ultimately impact business results. A learning leader from a training association said, "Strategic alignment indicates a *systems approach*. Great training can influence the culture and be a catalyst for change initiatives."

Conclusion

Strategic alignment is essentially the process by which an organization ensures that all learning initiatives support and align with the underlying goals and objectives of the company. Our research found that training professionals emphasize the indisputable position of strategic alignment as the most essential attribute of great training organizations. Without it, they say, training can be pointless, ineffective, and disappointing.

A company that has a mission to grow but doesn't prepare its employees for how to grow the business is going to have a hard time fulfilling its mission. This can happen within a department or for a corporation overall. Partnering with your internal client is critical to both understanding the target of the training and being able to effectively connect it to the business outcome. The more formal you make these connections, the more likely it is for the training to meet its objectives and, more importantly, move the key metrics.

In this chapter, we examined the following best practices for strategic alignment:

- Develop consultative partnerships with clients.
- Establish agreed-upon business objectives.
- Define performance success metrics.
- Customize training to meet the organization's needs.
- Adapt training to the organization's unique business or culture.

Strategic alignment is a vital part of everything we discuss in upcoming chapters. In Chapter 4 we explore diagnostics.

4

Diagnostics

Leaders of training organizations perform diagnostics in the same way as your doctor does: They assess current health, determine the cause of any problem, and recommend solutions to get to a desired state. In training, learning leaders perform diagnostics by assisting the current performance of the organization they support and determine whether the training solutions are achieving desired results. If the solutions are not achieving desired results, the learning leaders assess the root cause of the problem and prescribe actions to remedy or improve the situation. And, as with a doctor's first look, the objective is to determine what is performing as needed, what is not performing well, and what adjustments need to be made to reach the objectives.

Leaders of training organizations use a series of approaches, processes, or strategies coupled with previous experiences with other clients and initiatives to diagnose real problems. The quality with which a training organization uncovers the "true" needs or drivers of the gaps in performance is key to an organization's success. Some organizations rely heavily on the review of data to determine whether a client's training was as effective as it was designed to be. Diagnostics is important because it helps you link solutions to the needs of the business, and it helps you improve the probability of success, as well as the time it takes to deliver the training, increase the effectiveness of the training, and reduce the costs of doing it right.

Diagnostics is the bridge between understanding a client's needs and performance problem and delivering a set of requirements or specifications for the learning solution. It's important to comprehend that diagnostics doesn't end when you say you understand the problem. Diagnostics ends when you have a set of recommendations or specifications to deliver to the instructional design team. In a case where training can be procured from outside to solve a problem, the specs may be given to procurement and ultimately to the supplier. Specs must be delivered to whoever needs to be a part of the design of the solution or intervention.

Differences Between Diagnostics and Strategic Alignment

Essentially, strategic alignment involves training leaders working with clients to determine needs and understand client objectives. In addition, strategic alignment allows learning leaders to find problems so they can do diagnostics. For example, for a doctor to diagnose a patient's illness, he or she must interview the patient to understand pain and discomfort and then use data from tests to look for underlying symptoms and causes. Diagnostics is an activity that follows strategic alignment, where the leader triages problems related to the training organization's success in meeting client objectives. Think of it this way: You can't know what the root causes of the problems are if you don't understand the objectives. What makes diagnostics and strategic alignment different is that whereas strategic alignment determines needs, diagnostics determines what's keeping you from fulfilling those needs.

A large telecommunications company that was experiencing double-digit growth in revenues and employees provides an example of how diagnostics can help an organization impact the performance of the business. The learning leader was confronted with the problem that newly hired software engineers were being inserted into intact teams of product developers and expected to learn from their co-workers on the job. Inconsistencies in getting new hires up to speed and productive led to many quality issues, missed deliverables, and frustrations among product development managers and staff. To compound the problem, the company's growth required it to increase new hires by more than 2,000 software engineers per year—most of them right out of college.

To diagnose the problem, the leaders of the training organization met with client executives to understand the fundamental need of the business. They found that product development executives expected new employees to be productive much sooner than was actually happening. The time to productivity for new software engineers was much longer than what the software design organization expected—and needed. To compound the problem, the training leaders found that there was little budget appropriated for training new hires. The expectation was to get them trained quickly for little or no investment, basically through a few one-day workshops and then on-the-job training with co-workers. It was also found that the software engineers required knowledge of a very sophisticated software development environment, which included access to a proprietary product development methodology, as well as familiarity of the product architecture for which they would be developing code. These requirements were not being communicated consistently and effectively because the engineers expected to manage this communication had been hired just a few months earlier and had also not been trained properly.

After working with the client's leadership team and looking at the performance requirements of the software engineering role, the leaders of the training organization concluded that the fundamental objective was to quickly get newly hired engineers proficient enough to be placed into 5- to 10-person design teams without disrupting current activities—and, of course, to do it for the least cost possible.

To get to a solution, the learning leader had to deal with five key issues:

- The amount of training needed for each employee was estimated to exceed six weeks of in-depth classroom training, which posed a large expense, especially if the organization chose to use external suppliers.
- Much of the content was proprietary information. This meant it was impossible to source external instructors with knowledge and experience of the subject matter.
- The workload for trained and experienced software developers was so high that management of the product development groups had a hard time allowing employees to take time away from the job to do training.
- The new hires were being deployed into seven development centers, located in four locations in the United States, five in Canada, and two in the United Kingdom. Therefore, the training had to be replicated in multiple locations. Having new hires travel to a training center for six weeks was prohibitive.
- The training needed to be very hands-on, in labs with lots of instructor involvement.

Working with executives of the software design teams, the leaders of the training organization determined that the solution was to develop a six-week onboarding program that blended classroom, elearning, and virtual instruction. All the engineers began the training after one week of onboarding on human resources policies and procedures. They were then scheduled for a series of classroom- and lab-based programs delivered by internal subject matter experts to get them familiar with the proprietary development environment and product architecture. For the courses that consisted of nonproprietary content (object-oriented analysis and design and telecommunications protocols), distance learning was used, with one external consultant delivering to multiple locations in live virtual classrooms. This kept the cost of external training suppliers to a minimum.

The important learning from this example of diagnostics was that using a systematic approach to understanding the needs of the client, gaining an understanding of the causes and issues that affected the problem, and then looking for alternatives to find a solution returned the best solution for the best value.

Let's examine a training program that was being designed to help reduce the number of calls that were escalated from Level 1 support to Level 2 at a customer call center that was supporting the start-up of a new consumer technology product. By working with the client manager, the learning leader began the diagnostic exercise by pulling the data associated with calls from various call centers related to customer documentation. The analysis found that the highest percentages of call escalations (from Level 1 to 2) were coming from two call centers, both with inbound calls that were mostly non-English. The data showed that the call times for these two centers were substantially shorter than similar inbound calls to the English language call centers.

Using this data analysis, the client manager and the learning leader realized that the basic training for these groups needed to focus more on how the call center professional handled the initial receipt of the call. In all call centers, the first 30 seconds of engagement with the caller is the most important in understanding the problem and determining whether the customer's issue can be resolved quickly or whether it needs to be escalated for more detailed support. The client manager and the learning leader reviewed the current training program and compared it to the needs of the business. They found that in the non-English version of the call center professional computer screens, two initial screens did not have the appropriate information to help the call center professional solve the customer problem. They also found that the English program did have a review of these two screens and dedicated about 10% more time on the start-up of a new call with an inbound customer. Doing this simple type of data diagnostics of the problem led the team to redesign the screens for non-English calls, and they also updated the training solution. The improvements quickly led to a drop in the number of call escalations in the call center, saved money, and improved client satisfaction.

Linking Diagnostics and Content Development

Conducting diagnostics requires a consistent flow of information from the client, to the learning leader, and then to the content development team. As learning leaders work with clients to determine needs and to find out what problems need to be solved through training (strategic alignment), triage allows them to systematically understand the root causes of the problems, thus allowing them to determine workable solutions that they can communicate to the content development team. Diagnostics lays the foundation for designing training content, so that it can address the actual causes of performance gaps.

The challenge in performing effective diagnostics is to make sure content deals with the right issues—not with symptoms of problems. A training manager may be asked to recommend solutions to a client's business but ultimately is responsible for creating solutions within the control of the training organization itself. It's okay and necessary for the training manager to be able to determine when the root cause of a performance problem is not a training problem. Sometimes performance problems can be attributed to job design problems, as in the call center example we just examined. And sometimes a job or role must be re-engineered to make sure the process is correct. Training can then be done to update individuals on the new job expectations and requirements.

Training managers must be careful not to develop training that communicates bad techniques or processes. In the case of the call center, no amount of training was improving the performance or achieving the desired results because the training was teaching people to do the wrong things and use ineffective tools to get the job done. We find that this is frequently a problem in training organizations: teaching the wrong methods, processes, or responsibilities and expecting performance to improve.

The more you look into the underlying problems you are trying to remedy, the more you see key metrics that you would like to have in the reporting you do on an organization's performance. Since all training should be driven to have an impact on organization performance, the metrics used to design the training should be collected as part of the reporting on the program's effectiveness.

If training organizations execute diagnostics correctly, they can improve strategic alignment and content development and more effectively measure and affect results.

Case Study for Diagnostics: Performance Architecture

Let's look at a great example of how a corporation has systematically created a process for conducting organizational diagnostics. This process, called *performance architecture*, is managed within BB&T Corporation, one of the largest financial services holding companies in the United States. Based in Winston-Salem, North Carolina, the company operates approximately 1,851 financial centers in 12 states and Washington, DC.

BB&T's vast training experience has helped to identify that the key to meeting performance goals is not always training. The company has found that there are times in any organization when performance issues do not reflect a lack of employee knowledge. Although the appropriate remedy sometimes lies outside training, training departments and the clients they serve routinely opt for more instruction rather than seek the root cause of the problem. BB&T executives have turned the page on this mindset. "We've pushed back on the idea that the solution to every problem is more training," said Will Sutton, BB&T University manager. To address this need, BB&T, a six-time recipient of ASTD's BEST Award, developed a program that pursues a holistic approach to problem solving.[1]

Where "less is more" kicked in for Sutton was in determining when training efforts are appropriate and how best to approach needs beyond simply providing additional training to address performance improvement needs. The goal was to take a holistic view to system wide improvement, without wasting money.

Using Gilbert's Behavior Engineering Model, tailored to BB&T's specific needs to do performance analysis, the BB&T University design control group evaluates a wide range of options that consider all expectations. The group then responds to the business units with a plan that may or may not include training. Using tools such as gap analysis, it considers personnel skills, the corporate culture, the driving incentives, and all the data.

In one instance, the wealth division of the bank asked for training in eight new competencies. After careful examination, BB&T University made a case that the performance gap was more about motivation than about knowledge and skills.

As Sutton put it, "We wanted the business unit to understand that once individuals reach a core level of knowledge, with the wealth division staff having done so, simply layering on more depth in a topic does not enhance performance. I can show you scientifically that there's no correlation between additional knowledge and improved performance."

It didn't take long for the program to earn its stripes. The bank's wealth division, citing high performance expectations, had asked BB&T University to develop and deliver a broad new curriculum to train its employees on eight different competencies. In reply, BB&T University requested 90 days to examine whether training would actually solve the division's challenge.

Sutton said, "We found zero correlation between how the division's personnel performed on their assessments and their actual success as wealth advisors." Sutton's team felt that the wealth division's challenges reflected sales leadership opportunities, not skills or training deficiencies, and responded with a solution that did not involve the requested training.

What Sutton and his group are doing is nothing less than changing the mindset of management. Is it a hard sell? Not when all Sutton's team has to do is demonstrate that the solution identified through the performance architecture process saves the organization expense.

The Most Critical Diagnostic Practices

In the research for best practices in diagnostics, learning leaders have communicated five critical practices that training organizations must embrace to be a great training organization (see Figure 4-1) One of them stands out as the most important, with 95% of our survey respondents ranking it as critical. The following sections examine all five of these critical practices.

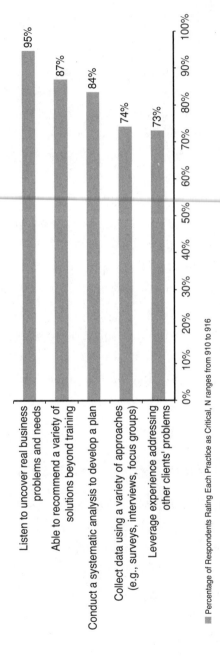

■ Percentage of Respondents Rating Each Practice as Critical. N ranges from 910 to 916

Figure 4-1 The Most Critical Diagnostic Practices

Listen to Uncover Real Business Problems and Needs

The most important diagnostic practice of great training organizations, according to learning leaders, is to listen to uncover real business problems and needs. Listening is about asking the right questions. It involves focusing on getting to root causes—not just the symptomatic response of client managers who believe they know what the problems are. Great training organizations listen to their clients and then dig deeply to truly understand what's driving a problem.

A director of training operations in a global pharmaceutical company said that too many training organizations make one vital mistake: "not taking time to really understand the client's needs."

Listening to uncover an organization's true needs is the first step in understanding a client's training requirements. Once the requirements are understood, a solution can be built around them. At a deeper level, good listening means asking questions that are probing, that are sometimes hard to ask, and that are sometimes harder to answer. This helps in accurately distinguishing the true need and then revising the requirements accordingly.

The following are examples of questions to ask when assessing training-related problems:

- **What is the business opportunity we are trying to impact?** Is the goal of the business, and ultimately the goal of the training, to improve the speed of service, reduce quality defects, improve client satisfaction, improve employee satisfaction, reduce customer returns, improve sales, or reduce lost sales opportunities? There can be many opportunities, but you need to get the right objective first.

- **What is the cause of the problem that you think this training may solve?** Understanding the true issue that is preventing someone from achieving an objective is critical. If the objective is to reduce quality defects, then it is important to determine the cause of the defects. Where is the greatest source of defects coming from, and what is causing the defects to occur?

- **Could there be any other causes of the problem that are unrelated to a lack of knowledge or skills?** Looking into other contributing areas is a good way to be complete and make sure every alternative solution is evaluated.

- **What has been tried so far to solve this problem, and with what results?** Past experience is a great teacher. Sometimes we don't know if the solution we are looking at will work without further testing. So look back in time to see if a particular solution has been tried. If it has been tried, how did it work?

One of the most important things to learn as you mature in performing diagnostics is the importance of data collection and management. Keeping good records for yourself and your successors, including results from previous training programs, could save the company a lot of money in the future when there are different staff members working similar problems.

John Hovell, senior manager at Lockheed Martin, said, "One action we take is to ask difficult questions."[2] Hovell tells us that an organization's ability to answer very difficult questions will directly correlate to the success of that organization. When they overlook these questions, organizations are not reaching their full potential. Mistakes are repeated, and intangibles are left to chance. Hovell insists that you must continue to ask, ask, ask...and listen!

Be Able to Recommend a Variety of Solutions Beyond Training

Great training organizations earn respect, build trust, and establish credibility with clients when they do not appear to be a "hammer in search of a nail." The more that training organizations serve as consultants and general problem solvers with solutions beyond training, the more value they offer to their clients. As a performance consultant, a learning leader is best positioned to consider nontraditional training solutions as part of the initiative. Sometimes the best solution is as simple as a communications campaign to make the staff aware of a problem. We call this *awareness training*. It can be the most cost-effective solution when people have the skills to do the job but are just not aware of a particular procedure or policy.

One senior vice president involved with learning services at a bank holding company said, "Properly assess performance improvement needs with appropriate and quality solutions that may or may not include training." Likewise, one learning and development manager at an agricultural company captured the spirit of this practice: "Great training organizations must be organizational problem solvers and consultants first and trainers second." In other words, great training organizations do not just create and deliver courses. They also facilitate learning and performance improvements in a broader sense through a myriad of other solutions. They are consultative in their approach, employing both diagnostic assessment and organizational development techniques.

A well-respected learning professional from a large technology company described his role on the sales team he supported as the performance ideas guy. He felt that his role was to come to every team meeting and listen for the barriers the team would experience when discussing how to achieve the goals set by the corporation each quarter. He made a clear distinction between developing courses (which were often required to solve some problems) and fostering the development of solutions to basic team performance inhibitors.

Conduct a Systematic Analysis to Develop a Plan

The key word here is *systematic*. Many organizations conduct assessments of needs for training, but we've found that high-performing organizations do this using a formal, systematic, and structured approach. Low-performing training organizations tend to conduct assessments using a rather informal and unstructured approach. A systematic needs analysis can include formal data collection, analysis of existing performance data, a gap analysis (the comparison of actual performance with potential performance) between desired skills and current competencies, and root cause analysis.

For every group, the design of the systematic approach will be different—almost custom. The key is to ensure that your company uses a complete and consistent approach before it develops any program. By conducting this type of analysis, training organizations can better identify critical needs and ensure the quality of the solution by maintaining records for future comparison.

A corporate training leader in a fluency company said that "only through systematic analysis" can it design an effective training program.

Anne M. Schwarz was once a package delivery person for UPS. She worked in many positions as she worked her way to becoming vice president, Global Leadership Development, of UPS. She still knows that before a training program can be designed and implemented, it is important to understand the business. She said, "Learn the business. Understand what the business is trying to accomplish."[3]

Schwarz did diagnostics and analysis which showed that parts of the company could respond to local needs more quickly if parts of the senior management team closer to the need were able to respond autonomously, as well as plan and market for localized specific needs. But those managers needed training in additional leadership competencies to be prepared for that trust.

So UPS transformed its largest U.S. business unit to consolidate and reduce the number of operating regions and give employees a greater ability to plan and market at the local level. The result was a one-week immersive training conference that responded to the needs discovered, offering senior leadership training in four competencies: finance, accounting, marketing sales, and leadership. It was designed to educate UPS leaders on how to effectively manage their businesses to make decisions using a more customer-focused approach, and it was the result of systematic analysis.

Collect Data Using a Variety of Approaches (e.g., Surveys, Interviews, Focus Groups)

Albert Einstein has been quoted as saying, "If I were given 60 minutes to save the world, I would spend 59 minutes defining the problem and 1 minute resolving it." Defining a problem is all about understanding it, and understanding comes from data. Similarly, training should be viewed as a solution to a problem instead of a part of a problem. In conducting diagnostics, training managers must recognize the need to collect as much data as possible in order to understand how training is performing and how training is impacting the business. This holds true no matter what the business or location.

A research and training manager for an airline said, "Robust data collection and analysis enables us to target our training with greater accuracy." But what does it mean for data collection to be *robust*? Because there is potential for measurement error in each instrument used, robust data collection means gathering data from different sources at various times for validation purposes. If all the data points in the same direction, you can have more confidence in the results, conclusions, and recommendations. What is particularly important here is making certain the data you base your recommended solution on is correct. Drill deeper. For instance, beyond an initial fact-finding interview, you may want to perform field observations or collect survey and interview data from a particular group. This allows you to better define and quantify the true nature and cause of performance or knowledge gaps.

For example, an organizational development manager at a transportation company described the company's data collection process, which is used to identify content for the leadership development program: "First, we did a Lominger card sort[4] with our top two levels of leaders to identify our leadership competencies. Then we interviewed each senior/executive leader to inquire about their top learning priorities for the managers/leaders they support. Lastly, we launched a survey to all employees asking them to provide feedback on various leadership topics (communication, feedback, recognition, etc.)—thinking about an ideal manager and their current manager. This feedback aided our gap analysis and helped shape our top priorities for the program."

Leverage Experience Addressing Other Clients' Problems

Great training organizations garner wisdom based on experiences working with a range of client organizations and learners. They recognize the signs of particular problems, know what to look for, understand what problems are common, and are aware of which solutions—learning or otherwise—have worked best in other situations. As much as we like to think that every training-related problem we encounter is unique, it's a good bet that someone has experienced a similar problem in somewhat similar means. A leader's ability to leverage his or her own experience, or even the experience of someone else in the network who may have seen something similar, is effective in determining best-in-class approaches to training. In addition, it's a huge opportunity to reduce the cost of diagnostics.

This is the essence of the service that Training Industry, Inc., provides. As one of several reliable industry experts and analysts that look across the market, Training Industry, Inc., looks for what works best in other organizations, spotlighting the practices it identifies in news articles, case studies, and best practices within the training industry.

Training Industry, Inc.'s focus, as well as that of the various industry associations, is to look for best practices in the industry and bring those to the forefront so others can learn from them. Searching for how others have approached a similar problem can save lots of time—and lots of money. It's about staying current—as doctors do when they read medical journals and IT professionals do when they read trade journals and relevant Internet blogs.

Learning from others helps dedicated business and training professionals get the information, insight, and tools they need to more effectively manage the business of learning. Such knowledge allows companies to quickly and accurately diagnose a problem and offer a broader range of solutions. Those who use the services of training organizations do not want collective insight to be wasted; they want training organizations to leverage their experience with clients, especially those whose problems resemble their own.

In addition to benefiting from outside information, a training organization should maintain institutional knowledge about solutions that have worked in other areas of the organization. A great approach to this that we have seen is a quarterly review session that a financial services learning organization holds. During this session, each team leader shares the strategy used to solve one problem for the team. The minutes and presentations are sent out to all attendees to be used as reference examples for future problems the team may face. The sharing of these case studies allows the different team members to see how their peers have resolved challenges across the organization. This way, when similar issues emerge, they do not have to reinvent the wheel. The organization could further improve this system by creating an archiving system for the minutes and presentations.

After all, the point of diagnostics is to understand a problem so you can design the right training to get results. It's about speed, efficiency, and effectiveness.

Conclusion

Great training organizations use a series of approaches, processes, or strategies coupled with previous experiences with other clients and initiatives, to diagnose training-related initiatives. The primary reasons it is important to handle diagnostics systematically are to increase the probability of success of training and to reduce the time it takes to get the right training delivered, to make sure it is effective, and to do it efficiently and cost effectively.

Conducting diagnostics helps training organizations link business objectives to their training and improve the probability of success.

This chapter explores the most critical diagnostics best practices:

- Listen to uncover real business problems and needs.
- Be able to recommend a variety of solutions beyond training.
- Conduct a systematic analysis to develop a plan.
- Collect data using a variety of approaches (e.g., surveys, interviews, focus groups).
- Leverage experience addressing other clients' problems.

Diagnostics lays the foundation for designing training content so that it addresses the actual causes of performance gaps. Chapter 5 explores content development.

Notes

1. "In Training, Sometimes Less Is More," http://www.astd.org/Publications/Magazines/TD/TD-Archive/2013/10/BEST-BBT

2. Hovell, John, "Managing Knowledge in High Performance Organizations," *Training Industry Quarterly*, Summer 2011, pp. 31–33.

3. Eggleston, Michelle, "UPS: Delivering Leadership Training," *Training Industry Quarterly*, Summer 2011, pp. 35–37.

4. The Lominger card sorting process works well with individuals or groups and provides a starting point for understanding one's portfolio of skills.

5

Content Development

Most people would agree that the single most important component of training is content. It is possible to manage a training experience well, deliver it in nice facilities, and have entertaining and engaging instructors without good content. But at the end of the day, the reason learners take training is to consume content—that is, to learn!

Many professionals in the industry still say that "content is king." We believe this is true. And we also believe that designing, creating, and delivering great content does not come solely through highly creative means. It comes through a number of best practices, or processes that, when done properly, can make a difference in good content becoming great content. These best practices are about making content relevant to the learner.

The concept of relevancy is revealed in the way some people like how a course is delivered and others do not. Different students can perceive the same content differently. It's not always because the content is either good or bad; sometimes it is because some people perceive the content to be more relevant and others see it as less relevant. This is one of the biggest challenges to training professionals: making content relevant to not just one learner but to a group of learners to whom the training is targeted.

Leaders of great training organizations understand the concept of relevancy very well. They understand that to be a great training organization, it is important to focus on the practices that allow them to provide content that is relevant and viewed as meeting the strategic needs of the business. One learning leader in a global business information firm said, "Without great content, everything else is irrelevant."

An important two-way aspect not to overlook here is that training must not only meet the needs of the business (and it should) but must also meet the needs of the learner. Both of these needs must be met.

So, in our definition of content development, we include both creating learning-related programs and keeping content culturally and technically up to date. Content development involves needs assessments, curriculum and instructional design for classrooms and media-based learning programs, and an ongoing process to eliminate out-of-date or inaccurate content. Great content is timely, easily accessible, consumable, useful, applicable, and based on real-world situations. An instructional designer must adapt instructional design strategies that help content adapt to the cultural and strategic change of the business.

So, how does a training organization go about creating great content that is credible and useful? It focuses on the following best practices of great training organizations.

The Most Critical Content Development Practices

In our research about what makes a great training organization, learning leaders told us that there are 10 distinct practices for creating great content (see Figure 5-1). Many successful organizations consider most of those practices, which we will explore in further detail, to be critical. Note that these are not the only practices that are important in creating great content, but they are the 10 most critical. If you do these practices, you are well on your way to being viewed as a strategic part of the business.

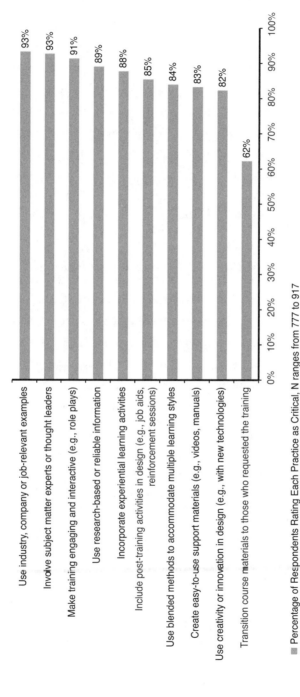

Figure 5-1 The Most Critical Content Development Practices

Use industry, company or job-relevant examples — 93%
Involve subject matter experts or thought leaders — 93%
Make training engaging and interactive (e.g., role plays) — 91%
Use research-based or reliable information — 89%
Incorporate experiential learning activities — 88%
Include post-training activities in design (e.g., job aids, reinforcement sessions) — 85%
Use blended methods to accommodate multiple learning styles — 84%
Create easy-to-use support materials (e.g., videos, manuals) — 83%
Use creativity or innovation in design (e.g., with new technologies) — 82%
Transition course materials to those who requested the training — 62%

Percentage of Respondents Rating Each Practice as Critical, N ranges from 777 to 917

Use Industry, Company, or Job-Relevant Examples

Research has shown that people learn best when they are able to associate information with their own experience and environment (i.e., *associative learning*). In short, they want training to apply to the real world and, more specifically, to *their* world. The more abstract or theoretical the training, the less learners will relate it to their own experiences or work performance. When examples provided in training are relevant and practical, learners can make direct connections to their own work more easily, and they are more likely to stay engaged with the content. This is why role-plays and simulation-based experiences in training courses are effective in knowledge transfer.

Involve Subject Matter Experts or Thought Leaders

Another way of making industry and company learning content especially relevant is by involving subject matter experts (SMEs), people who are experts in a particular area or topic, in the creation and delivery of content to their peers. Professional instructional designers must assertively seek out and engage SMEs early in the process of design to be sure content is relevant and aligned to the needs, and then they should engage SMEs again in testing the design to make sure it meets design requirements.

In some instances, actually allowing a SME to create content is useful when only that person understands the complexity and sophistication of the information being delivered. Content created by SMEs is called *user-generated content*. This form of content is often referred to as *informal content*, when it is developed without a professional instructional designer but made available for the purpose of getting critical information to the constituents in a very timely fashion. Many companies are incorporating user-generated content more than ever in order to increase the relevance of learning content and facilitate interaction.

Training Industry, Inc., and GP Strategies conducted a research study that examined how companies adopt, implement, and manage user-generated content in their training programs. These are the top three benefits that learning leaders identified for using user-generated content:

- Increased content and context relevance
- Increased capture of employee knowledge
- Increased content and context accuracy

As employees gain experience developing and using user-generated content, their ability to leverage the content for training and performance improvement will also improve. According to one training analyst with a nonprofit group, a critical role for a learning professional is to "integrate content with the participants' context, giving participants time to reflect and experiment with new behaviors and skills."

Both clients and learners trust experts, such as thought leaders and SMEs who have relevant knowledge and experience. One corporate training and development manager in a global technology corporation spoke highly of certain training organizations because their curriculum was specifically "developed by some of the best thoughts leaders of the day." Not everyone believes that experts have to design or author the content themselves, but respondents clearly feel more confident if experts are involved or consulted in some way in the creation of content.

Some people believe that having SMEs design content is risky because they are not trained in instructional design techniques. We advocate that learning leaders should support the use of SMEs by establishing strong relationships between them and the instructional designers and allowing them more latitude in how courses are designed and delivered. Research shows that the more they are involved, the higher the probability of the training being successful.

The data from the research study by Training Industry, Inc., and GP Strategies, confirms that organizations that involve SMEs during each stage in the content development life cycle are considered more effective. The study identified five primary practices that are critical for engaging SMEs[1] during the design and development process:

- **Clearly communicating expectations**—Learning leaders told us that the best ways to ensure that SMEs clearly understood expectations were to share the well-defined project scope and activities, define their roles and responsibilities, hold a project kick-off meeting, get the SMEs' input and agreement on the review cycle, create a formal plan with assignments, and establish a single point of contact and a communication plan for the SMEs.

- **Ensuring commitment to the project**—Learning leaders believe that they get the best commitment from SMEs when they feel their efforts and contributions are truly valued, when they receive credit for their work by having their names put in the materials, when they are recognized with monetary and nonmonetary incentives, when they are allowed flexibility in how they conducted their reviews of materials, and when their efforts are considered a factor in their potential advancement.

- **Cultivating a productive team dynamic**—The research found that SMEs were most effective when they feel they are a part of the team dynamic, which can be assured by maintaining communication through regular verbal discussions as well as through periodic emails and other communications when milestones are met. SMEs are also effective when their efforts and activities are posted in team environments, such as learning portals, message boards, and team meetings.

- **Effectively managing time on the project**—Time away from the job is one of the biggest concerns a SME has when getting involved in training. Learning leaders told us that effectively managing their time was best done by being well prepared for every meeting and encounter with SMEs, by engaging them for the right knowledge and complexity of content needed, and by holding meetings and reviews in the SMEs' own work environments.

- **Minimizing conflicting priorities between SMEs and learning and development teams**—Because SMEs have other priorities related to their primary job, helping them manage any conflicts is essential. Learning leaders told us that some of the best ways to do that are to make sure the leadership team has complete buy-in prior to assigning training milestones, realistically setting and communicating project schedules, and establishing an escalation process for scheduled conflicts.

There is an important aspect to consider here: Sometimes the content used for training is proprietary. The use of in-house SMEs is critical when disseminating proprietary information internally. No one from outside can do that. An in-house professional trainer can communicate the intricacies of experience and knowledge in the job. Imagine that it's like training the chefs at KFC franchises: Since the ingredients are touted as being "secret," you don't really want outside chefs doing the training. Another example of this is in telecommunications. When training software engineers about the next-generation technology being incorporated into new product design, who can do this training better than the design engineer responsible for developing the new technology? Think of Boeing, Microsoft, Apple, Coca-Cola, and any number of other companies where some secrecy is part of the product's brand.

Make Training Engaging and Interactive

Adults come to training with a variety of knowledge and experiences. If learners are not given an opportunity to connect what they know to the learning material, the trainer may find the training and the accompanying materials ineffective. Moreover, those trying to learn may consume the information, but true retention of the information will be lost in a very short time. For example, we all have experience in participating in one-way lectures, and we would probably all agree these may be efficient ways to convey information—but they are not always the most effective ways to learn, retain, and apply knowledge to the job. In fact, these instructional methods have been proven to be largely ineffective. The learners' engagement (i.e., participation and practice) is what allows them to experience how to use the knowledge on the job.

Lectures are well known for losing learners' interest and contributing to their disdain for future learning or training initiatives. A great example of how best to engage a learner is to think about a basketball player who needs to learn how to make free-throws at a higher efficiency level. A coach (trainer) can talk to the player about how to best shoot free-throws, showing slides and pictures of where to place the ball in his hands, how to properly follow through, when to bend his knees, and where to place his feet when shooting. But until the player goes out and practices shooting free-throws, the player will never truly improve his skills.

Simulations and role-playing are very effective means for engaging learners. They are tools for engagement and for getting learners involved in the experience of how to do the job right and also experiencing when they are doing it wrong. Without engaging learners, the time invested in the delivery of content is often a waste of limited company resources—and the time of all those involved.

Another great example of how to engage learners comes from the evolution of pilot training over time. Years ago, those teaching pilots how to fly abandoned the lecture approach and began to use flight simulators that allowed future pilots to operate in quite real-feeling circumstances. As a result of this training switch, far fewer crashes occurred. Numerous organizations have created similar environments in which they can immerse trainees so they stay better engaged and more thoroughly experience the steps toward their objectives.

There is another important reason that the use of role-playing and simulations can be necessary: the cost of failure. For instance, in the early days, the U.S. Army Air Force (USAAF) declined to use the simulators that were available at that time. Then, in 1934, the USAAF got the government contract to fly the postal mail. This meant having to fly in bad weather, for which the pilots had little training; in the first weeks, nearly a dozen Army pilots were killed and planes and mail were lost. In the future, other flying organizations looked to the budgetary reality of loss of equipment, lives, and materials being flown and decided that using simulation first was the way to go.

A great way to think of how to make training fun is through role-playing and simulations. As learners become and remain more engaged—and even enjoy themselves—they increase the probability of retention and application to real-world instances. One leader of an international marketing communications firm shared this observation: "Interactive discussion can be important to enable students to draw upon their own experiences, issues, problems, attitudes, affinities...since these will have maximum relevance. Role-play can be useful, but it needs to be appropriately constructed." Such interactive learning allows learning to be more self-directed, and it makes the learning more relevant to the students' needs.

One very interesting tool for making role-play fun is You Make the Call®, an interactive role-playing game designed for sales professionals. The product was created with the idea that the sales process can be a challenging and stressful experience. If you can make the learning of how to call on a customer more fun, the probability of success goes up for the sales rep.

A sales trainee who has been through numerous practice sales situations, working through resistance and achieving successful closes, is far more comfortable making a first call than someone who has only learned from a book or lecture. Designing courses for engagement and interactivity also implies that the instructor's role will include the *facilitation* of learning.

Another advantage of the role-playing experience is that it allows the learner to fail in a safe environment. Failure is a part of any learning process; we learn from our mistakes. But making mistakes on the job can be costly and detrimental for the business. So it's a good idea to allow a learner to fail in an environment where the risk of failure (and cost) is not as great as in the real job environment. Consider the training of a sales professional: Teaching a salesperson how to sell— or how not to sell—is probably better done first on a simulated sales call than in front of a customer. It's important to respect the time of customers, so using them as a part of the training process is not always perceived as a good investment of their time. Customers may not appreciate their time being consumed watching a trainee struggle through a sales call or even having a sales trainer or sales manager correcting them in front of the customer. In the case of high price-point products, the cost of failure could be even higher when having a sales trainee calling on a true prospective customer. The message here is that there are many risks associated with not having a salesperson properly trained prior to calling on a prospective client.

Use Research-Based or Reliable Information

Learning leaders told us that the use of research-based information—that is, reliable information backed up with data and sources—is more believable and trusted than other myths and opinions about how to best do a job. Leadership training is a great example of where we've seen the need for more scientifically backed and proven approaches to leadership practices. Great training content must be trusted and valued as being accurate and reliable. If a learner doesn't believe the content, then she probably won't engage it when she returns to the job.

Consider the difference between technical training and soft skills training. Technical training, such as IT, is fact based, involving technique and data. Technical content is generally perceived as reliable; it tends to rely on proven protocols and scientific truths. But soft skills training, such as leadership and management training, is often based on someone's belief about the best way to manage people. It becomes an expression of art. The more data you can bring to the experience, the more reliable and trusted the information will be.

In addition to gauging content quality by the experience and expertise of those involved in creating it, some respondents also evaluate content by the *process* through which it is created, such as how the research was done that goes into benchmarked solutions and how it supports the resulting documented best practices. Consider parts of the health care industry where constant statistics from research are routinely embedded in the problem-solving approaches. It's one thing to be told that this is the best way to handle a certain symptom or condition, but it's another to know that this is true 90% of the time or to know to watch for the 30% of patients who may respond differently and what to do when that happens. One team training consultant who particularly appreciates this best practice said, "Research is the most critical factor in content development—relying on scientifically valid sources instead of what some popular writer wrote. Long-disproven myths show up regularly in trainings I attend because the developers have just accepted something they had been told as fact instead of doing original research to verify sources." Integrity of research does matter.

Incorporate Experiential Learning Activities

Experiential learning is about individuals learning by actively doing and then analyzing and reflecting on their experiences. It relies on the initiative of the learner rather than the facilitator—focusing on one's own experiences rather than hearing or reading about others' experiences. With the increasing use of learning technologies, it is easier to make training experiential. A great example of this is in manufacturing training, where equipment operators are taught to operate expensive machinery while working in a simulated environment or while working directly with an instructor. The experience is monitored, and every activity is done with the instructor and student in unison.

Use Blended Methods to Accommodate Multiple Learning Styles

Training that is delivered using at least two different delivery methods is referred to as *blended learning*. The objective of blending multiple learning modalities is to enhance the learning experience for the student or to reduce the overall cost of delivery. Blended learning can reduce cost of delivery by allowing the part of the content that requires a live interactive connection between the student and the facilitator to be delivered either in the classroom or virtually through a live delivery platform; meanwhile, the part of the content that does not require a live interactive link is delivered via an online or asynchronous medium.

A common approach to blended learning is to provide online training for precourse conceptual information, such as terminology, models, protocols, and so on, and then following it up with a classroom experience to apply the conceptual information in practice. Microsoft, for example, delivers engineering training using a blended model called *Learning Paths*. Joetta Bell of Microsoft tells us that the company has had lots of success by creating Learning Paths into an organized, blended solution for engineers around topics of job roles. Microsoft has more than 100 different Learning Paths, which include curated content of courses, both online and in the classroom, bundled with articles, videos, and other types of informal content.

Learning Paths include about 60% to 70% informal content blended with 30% to 40% structured, instructionally designed courseware. This approach has allowed engineers to learn when they have time available, get the relevant information they need based on the topic or role they need to learn about, and get the information in an organized and efficient manner.

Various research studies by Training Industry, Inc., validate the importance of blended learning in all training contexts. In the 2009 study "Delivering Virtual Instructor-Led Training (VILT)," learning leaders reported using a less-blended mix of self-study, printed materials, and in-person instructor-led training (ILT), most often with virtual ILT. In a more recent study exploring training for first-time managers, learning leaders recommended that ILT be blended with self-paced online study with rich media content, live VILT, coaching, or live practice (e.g., role-plays) to obtain the best results.

As the adoption and use of immersive learning (e.g., simulations, game-playing, virtual classrooms or worlds) increases, more companies are starting to incorporate simulations and serious games with their current instructional methods.

Include Post-Training Activities in Design

Post-training activities (e.g., job aids, reinforcement sessions) provide opportunities to ensure that what was learned is applied—and applied correctly. These activities are a good idea because they increase the applicability of the training to the job. This improves knowledge transfer as well as performance on the job. It ensures that the trainees don't leave behind the knowledge communicated in the class at the end of the event. It increases the probability of performance improvement. It basically extends the training into the work environment and makes it more relevant.

Great training organizations are led by people who understand how others learn and retain information. Rather than view training as a single event, they understand that learning is a process that takes place over time—both formally and informally. Therefore, they build post-training activities into their pre-training design work to ensure that the training is supported and reinforced. For an example of post-training activities, consider the certification training for getting a captain's license for commercial shipping. The student is required to take an online course (through the cloud) that consists of videos and hands-on exercises. During the online course, the student is required to pass a test at the end of each module and then pass a comprehensive exam at the end of the online coursework. After the online work, the student must pass a physical (medical) examination to show that he or she is physically capable of doing the job. Then the student must complete a number of hours of experience, or on-the-job training, before being eligible to receive the final licensing credentials. Another example of post-training activities is the residency training that prospective medical doctors must complete after medical school. A student goes through four years of coursework and rotations, takes exams to qualify for the next level, does a year of internship and two to five years of residency (applied learning), and then can sit for the boards.

Create Easy-to-Use Support Materials

Performance support documentation during post-training activities helps sustain workforce performance improvements. It can detail both business process information and system transaction processing instructions through physical or electronic processes that are context sensitive. It can provide business workflow diagrams or even quick reference guides or cards that reinforce the training and help steer the learner toward expected results.

A practice leader of a prominent training supplier described the importance of performance support documentation by saying, "We are very focused on sustainable outcomes that do not rely on retention or memory, especially when the business requirements involve knowledge of a complex or technical nature." An example of such an information provider is Technology Research, Inc. (TRI), a company that provides market information and industry analysis to information technology vendors and purchasers throughout the world. TRI employs more than 300 analysts and annually publishes more than 15,000 research reports, addressing over 50 distinct subject areas (called *research programs*). The online knowledge repository comprises a standard set of knowledge units containing the executive summaries, abstracts, main text, graphics, tables, and charts that make up research reports. The repository is dynamic in that research reports are updated continuously. Knowledge units are indexed and linked for flexible access, and users can sequentially navigate from one to the next within a report, access similar units across reports (e.g., executive summaries only), or access particular units directly.

Allowing students to reference learning materials long after a course is completed allows them to refresh their knowledge and retain the information in the long term. Materials can be provided in the form of physical or electronic documents or through access to online libraries of training content and collateral materials. One learning leader in a global communications company specifically preferred "a good array of materials which are contextual, are not endless pages of text but have additional elements (ebooks, graphics, video files, PC-based information, Web references, etc.), and include *relevant* and appropriately detailed case studies."

A common practice in providing ongoing support materials is continuing to send articles, research, white papers, etc. after a class to continue the learning process. The challenge in this approach is that learning leaders must systematically manage content curation (the gathering and dissemination) as a process, which can be a bit of work. The advantage of doing this is that it brings the conceptual learning experience to the job and prolongs the learning experience, reinforcing retention and encouraging the appropriate behavioral change.

Creating support materials is also a rich opportunity for an organization to harvest mission-specific information that can be used to design proprietary training materials for reference. Think of the course materials as documentation the student can use back on the job. Making course materials available to the student online at and after the training is especially helpful.

Use Creativity or Innovation in Design (e.g., with New Technologies)

Innovation in design often has to do with using innovative technologies, including emerging ones, mobile technologies and devices, informal learning tools, online coaching, and communities of practice. Using innovation in design, especially through the use of technologies, is often about creating a "wow" factor for students. When this occurs, a student's depth of focus—or engagement—increases exponentially. The more deeply engaged a learner is, the more effective the content will be.

But being creative or innovative can also mean finding innovative ways to communicate a message. Leah Silverman from DesignbyLeah provides a great example of how to use creativity in the design of a program: She provides graphic illustrations created in real time during the training experience. While the class is being conducted, Silverman, a graphic designer and artist, captures the highlights of the learning activities on a large sheet of paper, creating a storyboard of the session that can be converted into a handout for each student.

A student can then post this handout on his or her office wall as an ongoing reminder of the key takeaways from the training course. This approach also supports the practice of creating easy-to-use support materials.

Fortunately, training organizations are not solely responsible for keeping up with new technologies. A learning solutions leader said that his banking organization's training unit keeps pace with industry tools and technologies for content development by developing and maintaining a small but robust network of external vendors.

Training Industry, Inc., and Intrepid Learning Solutions conducted a research study that examined how to effectively use technology-enabled informal learning, which highlighted the primary reasons companies choose to adopt this method. The top three motivations for implementing technology-enabled informal learning were to:

- Make content accessible to more learners.
- Increase learners' abilities to self-serve.
- Provide quick and easy ways to update and share relevant content.

In this study, when asked the topic areas for which technology-enabled informal learning works best, learning leaders reported sales, new employee orientation or onboarding, and product training as the top three.

To reiterate the relevance of emerging technologies in training, in a 2013 Training Industry, Inc., study, learning leaders cited mobile learning, online communities of practice, interactive learning, and immersive learning as the instructional methods they plan to use most often over the next year.

Transition Course Materials to Those Who Requested the Training

The transitioning of course materials to the clients who requested that the training be created is a best practice for content development that is practiced all too infrequently (63%). However, when utilizing third-party or sourced instructional designers, this practice could be essential. Owners of the intellectual property associated with courses want the control and flexibility to modify the content they own. They want to avoid becoming overly dependent on training outsourcing suppliers, or even internal training organizations, and want to take responsibility for their own content development once the basic course materials are created. One learning services manager in a global technology company specifically wants trainers to create "content built on open standards" that is "easy to update and maintain by the client once the initial project is completed."

Students also want access to the content they are learning about. They want to be able to take the content away from the learning environment so they can review it, refer to it, and find ways to make it a part of their jobs. Many learners like to own their own long-term learning experience. This is becoming truer every day, as demonstrated by students choosing to use a search engine when they encounter a business-related problem as opposed to waiting for the next class to find an answer to a problem or a solution. Going back to training departments for information has not traditionally been an option because training departments tend to hold on to the intelligence. A best practice of training organizations is to make the content more accessible and available after the learning experience. Or even to extend the learning experience.

This is one of the reasons knowledge repositories are becoming more popular. Such a repository provides a destination for learners to go after the experience, where they can get access to content in a usable and convenient way.

Conclusion

Effective design of highly valued content translates into better engagement with the learner. The more a learner is engaged, the more the learner will comprehend, retain, and apply. Engagement drives the motivation for trainees to retain and use what they have learned, for their own sake as well as the organization's goals. Use of SMEs, technology, innovation, creativity, and blending approaches are some of the techniques used to engage the learner in a more rich and meaningful experience.

The most critical content development best practices covered in this chapter include:

- Use industry, company, or job-relevant examples.
- Involve subject matter experts or thought leaders.
- Make training engaging and interactive (e.g., simulation, role-plays).
- Use research-based or reliable information.
- Incorporate experiential learning activities.
- Use blended methods to accommodate multiple learning styles.
- Include post-training activities (e.g., job aids, reinforcement sessions) in design.
- Create easy-to-use support materials.
- Use creativity or innovation in design (e.g., with new technologies).
- Transition course materials to those who requested the training.

In Chapter 6, we take a closer look at content delivery.

Note

1. For more information on best practices in engaging subject matter experts (SMEs) during a learning content development project, read the full report at http://www.trainingindustry.com/products/Research.aspx.

6

Content Delivery

Content Delivery is the execution phase of training. Delivery requires systematic organization of all the elements of facilitation. It is how content gets conveyed, or distributed, or even accessed. It's how content is made available. It is where all other practices associated with training design and development come to fruition. It is game time, when the show goes on. It is where all other training processes culminate, and the learner is engaged. Making sure you have great practices for delivery requires a focus on process execution—not just instruction. It's about making sure all aspects of the learning experience are addressed and orchestrated in a way that it meets design requirements.

When we speak of *delivery*, we are not just addressing those things that an instructor does. We are addressing all modalities of delivery, from classroom to online instruction. This chapter provides examples of each modality of delivery.

Delivery Modalities

To understand great training delivery, it is helpful to understand the various modalities of delivery. Obviously, delivery in a live classroom is the most common form of instruction. But delivery involves the conveyance of content in any form, whether it be live or online. The delivery experience for learners taking an online class on the internet is just as important as the delivery expectations for a live classroom with hundreds of students.

According to Kate Kibbee and Jeannette Gerzon at the Massachusetts Institute of Technology (MIT), there are five delivery modalities:

- **Classroom training with instructor**—An instructor delivers training to learners in the same location, and learners have the opportunity to interact and do hands-on learning or practice.
- **One-on-one tutorial**—An instructor provides individual instruction to one learner at a time.
- **Facilitated elearning**—An instructor delivers electronically while learners participate synchronously but in remote locations, such as webinars or webcasts.
- **Self-paced elearning**—Training is delivered asynchronously via electronic means, and learners set their own pace; content is delivered via computer, CD-ROM, Internet, etc.
- **Non-electronic self-paced learning**—The learner follows a course of study, setting his or her own pace, using materials that are generally in print (books or manuals), not via the Internet.

With the prevalence of elearning, video, virtual synchronous training, electronic performance support systems, mobile learning methods, and other training methodologies, delivery has become multifaceted. As discussed in Chapter 5, putting together the various facets into an integrated solution is critical to the execution of high-quality training delivery.

We've heard it said that a great instructor can make any training good. And we've time and time again seen a subject matter expert show up to a class with a set of PowerPoint slides, with the idea of conducting a training class. Of course, this is conveyance of knowledge. But it clearly is not what we have in mind when we think of great delivery.

Great delivery occurs when design and development are closely linked to delivery expectations. Unfortunately, all too often in our research, we have found organizations where developers and instructors do not operate in unison. And we have found situations where development has not properly defined expectations of the instructor or the role the instructor should play when facilitating. And oftentimes organizations do not define the delivery environment well, assuming that they need only specify online or asynchronous training.

Development does not have to define who the instructors should be, but it should profile or define the skill set requirements or knowledge that the instructor must possess to facilitate a program. A learning leader must make sure the delivery requirements are defined and then executed in the delivery processes. Without one hand feeding the other, the experience often is not optimized.

Continuity and consistency are critical. An instructor can hide poor design by being entertaining. But if design is not done properly, then delivery is vulnerable, and the ability to consistently reach a high level of training is compromised. A high level of training means that the trainer transfers knowledge and the students retain and ultimately apply it, resulting in improved performance and the needs of the business being met.

Like content development, delivery is often most associated with the actual training. The delivery of training is the conveyance of content to the learner. It's often the last opportunity for the training organization to manage the message being provided to the learner. As one training manager at a global technology company put it, "Delivery is the actual training. All else supports it." An employee development instructor manager at a Fortune 500 company emphasized the role of delivery as information dissemination: "If we don't get learning successfully into the environment, then nothing else we do matters."

Instructor Quality

Delivery is also one of the top three areas that companies feel needs improvement; in fact, it is a point of concern more often than any other process capability. Delivery is important in both disseminating information and forming lasting impressions, and delivery enhancements are likely to result in improved learner and client satisfaction. Influencing the learner's reaction to the content happens during delivery. We're talking about timeliness, and in the modality the learner prefers, or in which he or she learns best. In our research on the subject, even though the delivery of the training doesn't score highest in terms of importance, it is assumed that there is a certain level of efficiency when it comes to getting across a message.

Good delivery also depends on whether the learners like the trainer, the individual who delivers the training. Instructors with poor facilitation skills can negatively impact the experience for the learner. Or if the technology platform used to deliver content does not function correctly, the learner views the content as bad. It's like a great music event where the sound is just a little too quiet. The event loses its impact.

The Most Critical Delivery Practices

Successful companies most frequently use seven delivery practices (see Figure 6-1). Almost all successful companies view two of these practices as very critical (95% and 94%), and 46% to 89% of successful companies see the other five as critical. The following sections discuss the seven delivery practices that help make a great training organization.

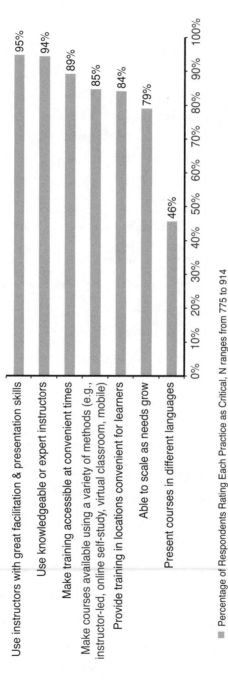

■ Percentage of Respondents Rating Each Practice as Critical, N ranges from 775 to 914

Figure 6-1 The Most Critical Delivery Practices

Use Instructors with Great Facilitation and Presentation Skills

In our study, 95% of respondents told us that using instructors with excellent facilitation and presentation skills is critical for a training organization to be great. The challenge here is understanding what great facilitation skills are and how to develop them. We contend that excellent skills are somewhat dependent on the type of content being delivered and the domain or industry vertical to which the instructor is delivering. A great instructor for IT may not necessarily be a great instructor for leadership training.

We consider these to be the most important facilitation skills:

- Being able to listen well to students' needs
- Being flexible to the ever-changing and diverse needs of the learner
- Being creative
- Being able to communicate and speak clearly and concisely, with good pronunciation
- Having a sense of logic and being able to solve problems using reasoning
- Being relevant to the business and industry you are teaching in
- Being tidy and having a good appearance
- Being influential while being respectful
- Being able to relate to participants on their level
- Being timely
- Being entertaining
- Being confident
- Being able to accept criticism
- Being compassionate and able to develop a relationship with students

One of the most common mistakes we make is to use subject matter experts as trainers without developing their facilitation skills. They can come across as experts in their field but lack the ability to convey knowledge or to engage learners.

The good news is that support for developing a subject matter expert's facilitation and presentation skills is readily available. One human capital development manager at a large public organization told us that we should promote the "proficiency of trainers as subject matter experts, instead of just trainers." Instructors also need to have interpersonal as well as presentation, communication, and facilitation skills to better engage the audience. One director of human resources at a specialty pharmaceutical company emphasized instructor versatility, adding that instructors need to have the "ability to deliver...in the best way," complementing the needs of the learner.

Use Knowledgeable or Expert Instructors

Learning leaders don't just expect instructors to deliver great, well-researched content; they also want instructors to be knowledgeable about the subject matter at hand. Many respondents insist on instructor experience and expertise—not only in the subject matter but also in the industry for which they are providing training. Let's assume that a facilitator has the facilitation skills necessary to pull off a high-quality training program. The facilitator also must have the depth and relevance to be able to make the learning real. He or she should be able to call on real-life examples that demonstrate or highlight the skill or subject matter covered in the program. Imagine learning negotiation skills from a master contract negotiator, or learning accounting from a member of the International Financial Reporting Standards (IFRS), or learning marketing from a marketing leader at Amazon. The examples those trainers use will be real, relevant, and meaningful to all participants in the program.

A learning leader of a global communications company said he desires "fresh and current trainers who have recent, real-world experience (and) who can talk credibly about first-hand experiences." This leader added that the trainers should be able to "relate either first- or second-hand anecdotes to let students understand how specific skills and knowledge can be effectively utilized to achieve desired outcomes."

Make Training Accessible at Convenient Times

As one learning leader in a health care company told us, training organizations "need to be able to provide training outside 'normal' work hours; [it is] difficult to continue to run a business when critical staff is attending training seminars." This is especially true in hospitals, where nurses are often understaffed but still need to comply with licensing regulations that require them to complete ongoing training updates. Fortunately, with technologies available that support asynchronous and self-paced instruction, scheduling issues can be virtually eliminated. Learners can take courses when their schedules permit, either outside or during their regular work day. On-demand, technology-enabled learning also allows employees to combine learning and work experiences by providing constant access to relevant information so it's available when needed. Human resource specialists have used this sort of ongoing learning themselves to keep abreast of changes in legal aspects, diversity issues, and trends that affect what they do. They can, in turn, provide learning that dovetails with the everyday work of specialists in their respective companies. As a director of training for an automobile manufacturer pointed out, truly convenient training is provided as close as possible to the time of need.

Furthermore, making training available at convenient times may not just be about the time of day. Training can also be delivered by creating courses in easily digestible, or "bite-sized," formats. One example is providing on-demand learning modules for a field repair tech. As a tech works through a problem at a customer location, he or she can access a variety of technical learning pieces, all less than a few minutes in duration, to show how to resolve problems similar to the one they are on site to remedy. A savvy training organization will make the content searchable and well organized, based on how the tech would look for things or the types of problems the tech is likely to run into. As one learning leader at an insurance company emphasized, "These days, my employees don't have four hours at one time to devote to training. [It is] better to have 30- to 45-minute modules that can be combined with others to make a training curriculum."

Make Courses Available Using a Variety of Methods

Remember the content development practice of using blended methods for different learning styles? High-performing training organizations provides courses that utilize a variety of methods of delivery (e.g., instructor-led, online self-study, virtual classroom, mobile, blended). Blended learning implies the use of multiple modalities in the same course. Making courses available using a variety of methods means using different delivery modalities within a curriculum. Whereas one course may be done as a pre-read technical manual, the next may be an online course, the next a practicum where all the students in a cohort come together for application training, and the following program a structured on-the-job program.

This delivery practice is about reaching people in the ways that align the content approach to the best way for the learner to consume it. This is about conforming content to the best approach to deliver, as opposed to being convenient to learning styles. Offering courses in a variety of ways not only gives potential learners the option to choose but can also help them consume content in the most effective way.

Provide Training in Locations Convenient for Learners

Providing training in locations convenient for learners doesn't necessarily mean elearning and mobile learning. It is increasing accessibility to training by bringing instructor-led classroom training closer to the learners' localities, or, with online training, directly to the learner's computer. With the advent of mobile learning, training information can literally go wherever learners go. This aspect is often about economics, convenience, and efficiency. Providing convenient locations for trainees means they don't have to travel and minimizes their time away from the job.

Be Able to Scale as Needs Grow

If an organization needs to train 100 times more employees in a particular course or needs to offer training to employees in various countries or regions, it must know that the training organization is poised to handle escalations in need. For example, Starbucks closed its entire business on Tuesday evening, February 26, 2008, to train 135,000 of its employees simultaneously on its new commitment to customers about service quality and upholding the uncompromising standards that have made Starbucks the world's leader in coffee retail. Not only was this a statement about the importance of developing the company's people, it was a tremendous undertaking in how to scale training to get the entire company on board with its new vision simultaneously. Scalability is about economies of scale. Great training organizations have the ability to train small numbers of employees or customers while also being able to train large numbers in a very short window of time. Scale requires clearly defined expectations, the ability to communicate consistently to a broad audience, and the ability to use resources throughout the organization.

Localize Courses to Audience Needs

For any type of communication, understanding the audience is essential for delivering the right message, in the best way possible. This includes addressing individual learning or delivery preferences, along with geographic, linguistic, or cultural standards. Customizing content or delivery methods to meet language or culture requirements is often necessary for multinational corporations. While some cultures are hierarchical, others are democratic and participatory— which means that learner involvement or peer-to-peer interaction may be comfortable for some learners but not others.

A global leadership development program must focus on the appropriateness of content for all cultures. But it is also critical that these same differences that are always considered when using words and images, examples, or people in programs be considered when choosing modality for delivery. Debating how effective a feedback strategy is with your manager or someone senior to you in a course may be fully acceptable in Canada, but in many Asian cultures, that technique would not work as the challenging of superiors may not be as readily accepted. In addition, courses should be taught in the language that the audience prefers to ensure the proper dialect and vocabulary level of participants.

Conclusion

This chapter describes the most critical delivery best practices:

- Use instructors with great facilitation and presentation skills.
- Use knowledgeable or expert instructors.
- Make training accessible at convenient times.

- Make courses available using a variety of methods (e.g., instructor-led, online self-study, virtual classroom, mobile, blended).
- Provide training in locations that are convenient for learners.
- Be able to scale as needs grow.
- Localize courses to audience needs (e.g., culture, language).

Chapter 7 explores administrative services: managing the end-to-end experience of learning.

7

Administrative Services

Training administration is about managing and controlling the end-to-end experience of learning. It begins with the strategic activities associated with working with clients to identify needs: planning when and how solutions will be developed and fulfilled; scheduling programs and students, registration, and material fulfillment; and planning other back-office support functions such as financial management, marketing and communications, assessment and testing, vendor management, and tuition reimbursement.

You can have great content, great instructors, great technologies, great classrooms and facilities, great materials, etc., but if the fundamental processes associated with the experience a learner goes through before accessing the training and after the training is completed are not done properly, the student's perception of the quality of training could be negative.

For a training organization, there are many opportunities to interact with a learner before, during, and after the actual training occurs. If any of the interactions is flawed, the learner's perception of the entire experience may be that the training was not good or that it was not effective. Managing the administrative experience requires credibility, efficiency, and effectiveness. Some believe that administrative processes should be transparent to the learner, meaning that the more effective administration is, the less visible it is to the learner. The idea is that if administrative activities are too visible to the learner, they get in the way of the learner's experience.

You may choose to debate this, based on the idea that technology can be used as a differentiator in how a student accesses training. This, by nature, means the administrative activities cannot be transparent. Differentiating the administrative experience involves using non-learning-related processes to wow the learner. But not executing those processes properly could negatively impact the overall quality of the experience.

While administration is often referred to as "the back office," many learning strategists believe that administration is, in fact, the lifeblood of an efficient and effective training operation. It includes the logistics of integration, often technology enabled, of many business processes and resources into an operation of transparently managed activities.

Ironically, only 23% of the respondents in our research viewed administrative services as a critical process capability for training organizations to be viewed as high performing. Instead, they view administration as a support function that helps facilitate the more critical and core elements of training. Yet our experiences tell us that *administrative services are the bedrock of a great training organization, providing feedback and making sure programs are scheduled and delivered as planned, with little disruption to the student or instructor.* In short, administrative services provide the logistical infrastructure that enables training to happen. The irony of administrative services is that if the administrative personnel are doing their jobs well, you hardly know they are doing their jobs. So, when it comes time for organizations to look at budgets and costs, administrative services is one of the first places where they seek to get leaner.

It's difficult to talk about great training administration without dealing with the issue of cost. The students see content and delivery most prominently; it's what they view as the most important components of the training experience. But the administration of services is what makes it all work. It's like the foundation that holds up a building.

If you take it out, the building crumbles. But no one talks about how beautiful the building is while looking at the foundation.

There is no general rule on how much an organization should spend on training administration compared to the amount of training delivered. The investment in administration often varies based on how technologically oriented the company is. Typically, high-tech companies spend a lower percentage of their total training budget on administrative activities than do their counterparts in companies such as hospitality and services companies. We do not contend that this is either good or bad, just that the more technology enabled a company's culture tends to be, the more it uses technology in the administration of training.

The Most Critical Administrative Services Practices

High-performing training organizations consistently demonstrate that they are process oriented and focus on managing day-to-day activities with exceptional detail. Being process oriented allows them to continue to find ways to improve efficiency, as they execute five main practices. It's important to note that the use of technology often enables cost reduction, but it is not a requirement. The use of technology is dependent on volume, which means that to justify the cost, there must be enough volume of usage to warrant the up-front cost expenditure and to amortize its cost over a period of time. The use of technology is not a prerequisite for excellence in administration—or in any of the other capability areas.

Of the five administrative practices mentioned most frequently, the top three relate to tracking and organizing learners, instructors, and course information (see Figure 7-1).

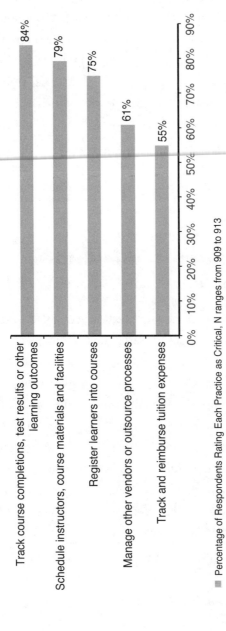

Percentage of Respondents Rating Each Practice as Critical, N ranges from 909 to 913

Figure 7-1 The Most Critical Administrative Services Practices

Track Completions, Test Results, or Other Learning Outcomes

At a basic level, training organizations need to track who took which courses and compile data on what they learned. Without such data, a training organization will not be able to effectively report on the performance of the training program. In fact, perhaps because of its link to the more critical reporting and analysis capability (covered in greater detail in Chapter 9), this practice is the highest-rated of all administrative services practices. The key to tracking is data management. To better plan for future requirements, it's important to understand what has happened in the past—for example, to know who has completed training so you will know who needs it in the future. It's about knowing how to schedule future programs to be efficient. The other keys here are compliance, liability protection, and funding allocation.

Schedule Instructors, Course Materials, and Facilities

Once training is designed and learners have been registered (or self-selected) for courses, the process of logistically managing instructors, materials, and facilities requires efficient coordination of resources. The objective is to make sure all come together at the right time. The objective of this practice is to make sure you utilize resources efficiently. A huge waste area for training organizations is to have low capacity of classrooms, thus wasting dollars on instructors not being fully utilized or materials that get thrown away. An even worse area of waste is students showing up for training and the materials or facilities not being ready. An organization spends a large amount on facilities—a fixed expense—so if a training organization has dedicated classrooms, it needs to get maximum utilization from those rooms. Many companies are now sourcing classrooms through external organizations, such as classroom facility providers, hotels and conference centers rather than maintaining their own for the purpose of minimizing fixed expenses of real estate. And of course there is a huge trend of moving classroom training to virtual delivery to minimize the need for fixed real estate..

Register Learners into Courses

Once a course has been created and scheduled, enrollment should be easy and comprehensive, triggering all the additional logistics (e.g., course materials) that may be associated with each learner. Many organizations use open enrollment, allowing learners to schedule themselves for upcoming classes. This is not a best practice. High-performing training organizations utilize a more direct scheduling approach (called *targeted enrollment*), where they preschedule students for upcoming programs based on needs—the needs of the learner, the needs of the business, and learners' roles in the business. Joetta Bell, senior curriculum and operations manager at Microsoft, says that their organization has shifted to a targeted enrollment model for training software and test engineers. The objective of this shift was to make sure the right engineers were getting the training they needed, based on business initiatives. Engineers are scheduled for training in intact teams, based on the most effective time for the engineer to receive the training. The training is designed based on the specific needs of the learners.

Red Hat preschedules managers into its Leadership Academy as part of its targeted enrollment that allows for scheduling intact teams and key resources into programs, based on how the business needs them to be trained. The best practice here is not about making registration easy to do. It's about scheduling the right people for the right program at the right time so the investment in training reaches who it needs to reach and when.

Manage Other Vendors or Outsource Processes

Our studies have found that virtually every company outsources some part of its training function. Whether it's as tactical as using a hotel for classrooms or outsourcing all the sales training activities to a sales training company, every company must be astute in managing suppliers. When clients demand specific areas of expertise or delivery, or when they have other requirements that cannot be met by internal resources, the sourcing of external suppliers can be critical. Clients can solicit training suppliers for almost any training process. The relationship they choose to have with a supplier is dependent on how strategic the need is for the process they choose to source. Sometimes the relationship with a supplier is as simple as delivering a course on a given day. Sometimes it's a large-scale engagement where the supplier takes over the management of the process(es) for several years.

For example, Boeing utilizes a training supplier to manage its registration and scheduling services for employee training. This supplier manages online and telephone-based registration throughout the world from one offshore call center. Boeing adopted this model in order to utilize a company that specializes in this type of service so that internal staff at Boeing could focus more effort on managing the strategic needs of the business.

High-performing training organizations are good at integrating the capabilities of external suppliers with their own internal capabilities and then leveraging their services with their own client base. Since training organizations cannot necessarily perform every learning service, they must develop the capacity to manage relationships with other service providers and then align those providers' services with the priorities of their clients. The objective of this practice is to have high-performing organizations utilize vendors in a strategic way, so they get the most performance from them at the best market value. They want to have low turnover among long-term suppliers, have good rapport, and have the suppliers work diligently to make sure needs are met.

Track and Reimburse Tuition Expenses

Some organizations offer their employees the opportunity to be reimbursed for educational or professional courses that they take beyond their corporate training.

Organizations should collect data on tuition expenses to evaluate whether the reimbursement programs have the intended effects—and are worth the investment. This information can also be used to help negotiate discounts at certain institutions and can ensure that programs are being administered correctly.

Not all companies offer tuition reimbursement, and those that do often manage the program outside the training organizations (e.g., in human resources or finance departments). Since these programs are not common in all training organizations, doing tuition reimbursement well is not deemed as crucial as some other administrative practices. Tracking tuition reimbursement is not solely a financial activity but a means for understanding where the resources skill sets are being developed and how to leverage talent for future assignments. This links back to ensuring strategic alignment.

Conclusion

Administrative services are the bedrock of a great training organization, providing scheduling, tracking, and feedback and ensuring that programs are delivered as expected, with little disruption to students or instructors.

Transparency is essential in managing administration in a great training organization. The more transparent the processes are to the learner, the more effective they are. The inherent costs of managing a training organization are considered non-value-added costs and will always be targets for cost savings. But these costs are critical in making sure training is effective and efficiently delivered. Great training administration is about enhancing the learner's experience. Any program can experience adverse effects from poor administrative services.

Five best practices of administrative services are discussed in this chapter:

- Track course completions, test results, or other learning outcomes.
- Schedule instructors, facilities, and materials.
- Register learners into courses.
- Manage vendors or outsourced processes.
- Track and reimburse tuition expenses.

Chief among these practices are that training organizations should proactively register learners into training, based on business needs (as opposed to allowing learners to openly register themselves), track who completes the training, and compile data on what the students learned. Without such data, a training organization will not be able to effectively report on training program performance and make improvements to the next set of learners. This is the highest rated of all administrative services practices because of its link to the critical measurement and certification and reporting and analysis capabilities covered in the next two chapters.

8

Measurement and Certification

Donald Rumsfeld, the former secretary of defense of the United States, once stated that there are "unknown unknowns"—things we do not know that we do not know; there are "known unknowns"—things we know we do not know; and there are "known knowns"—things we know that we know. His point was to tell the country that before making a critical decision (such as going to war), it is important to move from the state of unknowing to that of knowing—and being absolutely sure that we know that we know.

This logic applies to learning leaders as well. It is the nature of the training profession to assist learners from moving from the unknown to knowing. Some call this the *concept of knowing*. This has been a very important pedagogical concept for many years. It's about answering the question "How do you know that you know?" For business leaders, it's about answering the question "How do we know that our employees or customers know what we need them to know?"

There are three critical components to the concept of knowing, which drives measurement and certification:

- **Control**—Control refers to the idea that the more we know we know, the more we can control a process—or the more in control a process is—thus helping in controlling quality, budgeting, and expense management.

- **Demonstration**—Demonstration refers to the idea that to reach the state of knowing, a learner must be able to demonstrate knowledge and ultimately performance. We cannot know that an individual knows all aspects of a job until she has demonstrated that knowledge.

- **Risk**—The third component of the concept of knowing is risk. The more a learner knows, and the more we know that she knows, the less risk there is in putting that person in a job where failure could be catastrophic or of high consequence—either to herself or to the business. For example, in health care, we *must* know that a medical doctor knows all aspects of her job. Or in the case of airline pilots, it is critical that we know that they know all aspects of the job. We can't afford for them to fail.

The concept of knowing is the foundation for measurement and certification, which is critical in creating high-performing training organizations. Those who understand this concept and create systems and practices to make sure they know that their employees (or customers) know what they need to know will drive their organizations from being tactical training organizations to being highly strategic.

Measurement allows you to understand what you need to know. It helps you know how your organization is performing at any given moment. It also helps you know how an individual or a constituent of a training organization is performing. Certification is a mechanism for demonstrating what or how much someone knows.

Measurement and certification are also important in determining where and how to invest in certain areas of training. Measuring activities and results from training and recognizing individuals who have demonstrated that they know the subject matter they are being trained on are fundamentally important aspects of moving from unknowns to knowns.

A leader in a high-performing training organization must understand the issues that confront the business and must get the information needed to make intelligent, well-thought-out decisions about what needs to be done in the future. This is where measurement, certification, analytics, and diagnostics all meet. Each plays a part in making sure that training is strategically aligned with the objectives of the business.

Certification takes us to the state of knowing what someone knows. It addresses the questions "How do we know that a student has the skills to do the job?" and "How do we know that a student is proficient?" It also deals with the question "How important is it that we know that a learner has gained the knowledge or mastered a task?" Organizations that perform at very high levels have demonstrated that this state of knowing is critically important for financial reasons—not just for the security of knowing, but for making sure that dollars are spent where they need to be spent.

Measurement as a Strategy

The fastest way to success is to develop a plan and systematically stay the course to achieve the desired results. As training is an important means to improving the performance of a business, having a measurement strategy is critical to systematically making sure that improvements are made on processes that need to be improved. Improvement is successful only when it is in areas where the business needs it the most.

High-performing training organizations do not just measure activities and outcomes; they systematically measure what is important to measure related to how a process is performing. And they focus their efforts on the things that get the business the most return. For example, if the focus is to measure the volume of training activity but not measure how training impacts a client's organizational performance, you may never make any sustainable improvement to the business. Suppose that the single most important metric to a training organization is the results of end-of-class evaluations from training programs. A learning leader may believe that getting an average rating of 4.5 overall on a scale of 5 indicates that the students value the training program, the instructor is doing a great job, and the facilities and materials are well received. However, this strategy for measurement doesn't take into account how the client of the training—that is, the executive who oversees the operations of the line of business where the employees are employed—views the training. Many organizations in today's business process outsourcing (BPO) market make this fundamental mistake, and training companies' service-level agreements are based on end-of-class evaluation scores but not on whether the employee changed behavior and applied the skills on the job.

Billions of dollars are spent each year on employee and customer training. Organizations are becoming keenly aware of how important it is to measure progress, results, and ultimately, if possible, the all-important return for the training dollar.

Good measurement, well done, can affect the bottom line—and it can also be complex, and its accuracy can be elusive. Helping corporate leaders see and feel the value of training is vital to sustaining programs, but accurately measuring learning investments is its own reward.

Let's look for a moment at some of the things organizations can and do measure.

Kirkpatrick's Four Levels of Evaluation

Donald L. Kirkpatrick, a former professor at the University of Wisconsin, established in the 1994 version of his book *Evaluating Training Programs* what have come to be industry standards in organizational measurement. The four levels of Kirkpatrick's evaluation model essentially measure:

- **Level 1–The reaction of students**—What they thought and felt about the training. This measure can be obtained through subsequent verbal or written reports given by delegates to managers back at their jobs. It's easy to gather and can be done quickly, and it is important that people give a positive impression when relating their experience to others who might be deciding whether to experience that mode and method of training.

- **Level 2–Learning**—The resulting increase in knowledge or capability. Tests can be administered before and after the training. This can be highly relevant and clear-cut for certain training, such as training on quantifiable or technical skills, but it is less easy for more complex learning, such as attitudinal development, which is famously difficult to assess.

- **Level 3–Behavior**—The extent of behavior and capability improvement and implementation or application by trainees. Observation and interview over time can be used to assess change, the relevance of change, and the sustainability of change, though the measurement of behavior change is less easy to quantify and interpret than the "reaction" and "learning" evaluation levels.

- **Level 4–Results**—The effects on the business or environment resulting from the trainee's performance. Thanks to normal management systems and reporting, many of these measures may already be in place, but it is important to identify and agree on the accountability and relevance with the trainee at the start of the training, so he or she understands what is to be measured. Individual result evaluations are not particularly difficult, but across a large organization, they become much more challenging. They can be done, and, when done properly, can lead to clear accountability—that Holy Grail of business measurement, the return on investment (ROI).

All the Kirkpatrick levels of evaluation can and should be used for a full and meaningful evaluation of learning in organizations, although their complexity, and even cost, can increase as administrators progress upward to the "results" level.

The Use of Isolating a Variable to Better Understand the Impact of the Program

In evaluating the effectiveness of a new training program and determining whether the design meets the desired results, delivering the program in a controlled environment or to a controlled study group is a good technique. With this technique, one group receives training while a similar group does not receive training. The difference in the performance of the two groups is attributed to the training program. When this technique is properly set up and implemented, control group arrangement is the most effective way to isolate the effects of training.

This technique is sometimes an overlooked strategy in evaluating the effectiveness of a new training program. Many organizations use a different technique: running a program to a select audience and evaluating the audience's perception of the training after the fact. This technique does not isolate differences and does not take into consideration the impact of the training on the business—just the impact on the learner.

Anything That Can Be Done Right Can Be Done Wrong

While measurement done correctly has proven value, it is also possible to make mistakes. Here are a few of the things that can go wrong:[1]

- **Failure of alignment with critical stakeholders**—In the quest to satisfy senior executives about that elusive ROI, many training organizations assume that those leaders are eager just for hard-line, quantifiable results such as revenue growth or a win rate for sales. It's best to check first. When the leaders believe their people, anecdotal evidence about how learning has impacted performance may be more compelling.

- **Building plans that are too elaborate**—Setting clear priorities and assigning specific roles to the right people can help companies simplify for more effective execution.

- **Defining measurement approaches that cannot be practically executed**—The question to always ask is "Can we really achieve these measurements?"

Credentialing

In the professional and corporate market, a credential is an important attestation of qualification, competence, or authority made by a qualified source of authority. A commonly used credential can be a diploma, certification, badge, or clearance. The value of the credential lies in how well it is recognized by others in the market as the credential of choice and the level of rigor it takes to complete the credentialing requirements.

In the legal profession, lawyers earn a valuable credential that carries with them through their career. Passing the bar exam allows a lawyer to call himself an attorney and practice law. In trade industries where government regulations are associated with who can practice in that industry, a professional credential is required to receive income for performing that service. Consider the construction industry: An architect must complete a bachelor's degree in architecture, complete an internship, and successfully complete the Architect Registration Examination. A builder must pass the testing requirements to be a general contractor, and an electrical contractor must pass a test to be an electrician and a contractor. All these credentials are recognized by the industry as a whole—most importantly by those who contract for services of these professionals.

Medical practitioners must also have credentials in the form of licenses issued by the government of the jurisdictions in which they practice, which they obtain after receiving suitable education, training, and/or practical experience. Most medical credentials are granted for a practice-specific group. They may also be withdrawn by their holders in the event of fraud or malpractice. Typically a person who holds a credential must receive continuing education validation and renewal in order to continue practicing.

Certifications

Certifications are another form of credentialing, but they are generally less stringent than professional credentials. A certification is an excellent way of measuring and confirming an individual's progress through training by being certified by an outside third party.

IT professionals, for instance, must continually upgrade their skills to stay current in their fields and keep themselves marketable. The single thing that distinguishes an IT professional when he or she is competing with peers is certification. A third-party endorsement proves that an individual really knows what she says she knows, and that goes a long way toward keeping her on the shortlist. Not only do certifications help an IT professional stand out from the crowd, they let everyone around know that individuals who hold them are committed to their cause and have invested their time and monetary resources in staying at the top of their game.

Beyond the development of technical skills, IT certifications often produce more well-rounded employees. For example, according to a 2009 CompTIA survey of 1,185 certification holders, nearly 1 in 4 said they believe they have better customer skills because of their certification. More than one-third (37%) feel that certification enhanced their productivity directly, but the bigger positive impact to productivity stems from more insightful problem solving (47%). This is a situation where the employee may not fully realize the benefits of the knowledge gained from certification prep, but it certainly has an impact on the workplace.[2]

Badging

Everyone wants to be recognized for achievements. Certifications, degrees, and job titles have long been badges that signify a person's position of responsibility or professional accomplishments. But social media has demonstrated that business professionals long for other forms of recognition. The number of followers on Twitter is a status symbol for someone's importance, the number of Facebook friends indicates how much someone is valued by others, and the number of likes to what someone publishes demonstrates the value of the message. In the corporate setting, receiving a Black Belt not only demonstrates how much training you have completed but also that you have demonstrated success in managing projects. All these are forms of social badges. Personal learning environments provide a new world to create more of these forms of recognition. Badging is growing at such a rate that our challenge will be determining how to vet out which badges are acceptable and valued in various environments.

While badging is not strictly a function of a training department—many badges are earned for work-related accomplishments rather than from traditional learning—trainers are wise to endorse and encourage them within recognition activities (e.g., participation on a project, completion of a milestone like longevity of service, recognition of an award). Awarding badges is, after all, consistent with a climate of achievement championed by every learning department and CEO. Trainers need to recognize that people are incented in ways other than learning.

Conclusion

Measurement of training programs can have a positive revenue effect for organizations. Kirkpatrick's four levels of evaluation have come to be industry standards in organizational measurement. Performance success metrics can help tell a business manager the value of the training and can facilitate measuring after the fact to see the impact. Isolating a variable can also help to better understand the impact of a program. Measurement can be done incorrectly or correctly, so it's best to avoid assumptions or getting too elaborate or even aiming for unachievable measurements.

Credentialing, certification, and badging are ways of identifying and acknowledging accomplished skill levels through varied means of confirmation.

Having considered measurement and certification, in Chapter 9 you will learn about reporting and analysis.

Notes

1. Carder, David, "Six Critical Measurement Mistakes and How to Avoid Them," *Training Industry Quarterly*, Spring 2012, pp. 28–31.

2. Greenspan, Daniel, "The Real Value of IT Certification: Facts, Figures, and Perceptions on IT Certification from IT Managers and IT Professionals," *Netcom Information Technology* white paper. October 27, 2009.

9

Reporting and Analysis

An organization's abilities to define the proper metrics for business processes, collect appropriate data in a cost-effective manner, report the data, and make strategic recommendations on how to improve the business form a foundation for research and analysis.

"The purpose of training is to create positive and financial improvements within the company. It is important to determine if the desired results are produced after training," said a training manager from a regional real estate title company. A senior vice president of marketing, and a client of training organizations at an automotive parts distribution company, observed that "in tough economic times, all companies are looking for ROI [return on investment] on all projects."

Reporting and analysis helps decision makers and training organizations decide how and where to invest in specific training as they move forward. Basic reporting and analysis capabilities allow leaders of training organizations to get the credit they deserve for the results they actually impact. Without reporting and analysis, clients of training organizations rely on anecdotal, rather than hard, evidence to determine the effectiveness of training.

What to measure regarding performance is a challenging question. For years, the focus has been on measuring the learners' retention of content. The thinking has been that if a student learned and retained content, that must translate into improved behavior on the job. Therefore, many training organizations have focused on

measuring or evaluating students' behavior at or following the classroom experience. We have learned over the past few years that this
is not the case. We have to focus more on evaluating how a learner's
behavior impacts the business to determine the true effectiveness of
training.

The focus for high-performing organizations is on measuring the
performance of the business to determine whether the training had
true and measureable impact. The paradigm shift for most learning
leaders is to recognize that if learners' performance improves, there
must ultimately be improvement in the business, as long as the training focuses on the right things. Oftentimes training gets positive feedback from students but has no measureable impact on the students'
performance on the job. Also, we find that after training, learners'
knowledge of a subject may improve, but there is no recognizable
impact on the business. Each of these scenarios suggests that a training event was positive for the learner but not aligned to the needs
of the business. Reporting and analytics help us understand whether
training is having an impact on the learner and then ultimately on the
business. As learning leaders, we must always be asking whether the
training we are providing truly meets the needs of the business.

An example of performance success metrics can be seen in manufacturing training. Consider the scenario of a production department
experiencing quality problems of goods coming off an assembly line.
When a learning leader is brought in to look at the training for production line workers and is asked how training can improve the performance of the production line, the learning leader should look to
the metrics the production department is using to indicate that performance is below expectations. It may be that the number of units
produced is below standard, or there may be excessive quality defects
coming from the line personnel. Such information tells the learning leader that critical training is needed to improve quality and/or
increase the number of units expected. Training would be developed

to specifically address the causes of each. The training leader may choose to use Pareto analysis to determine the root cause of the problem and design training to deal specifically with the cause.

After the training occurs, the learning leader allows the personnel to incorporate their learning into day-to-day activities. Then he or she measures the production line's performance after the fact and compares it to the pretraining performance. The learning leader can then see the level of impact the training had on the business. This demonstrates the relationship between understanding the business problem by working with the business leader, designing mission-critical training specific to the needs of the business, identifying the specific performance success metrics that will tell the business manager the value of the training, and facilitating measurement after the fact to see the impact.

A vice president for education services at a software company put it this way: "Training organizations need defined performance success metrics—not just training metrics but business transformation metrics as well. This will show the success and value of training programs."

While reporting and analysis can provide useful information on specific initiatives, the results can also be aggregated to evaluate training providers and to help make decisions about future training projects and budgets. Given the importance of proving overall value, it is particularly important to master the art and skill of reporting and analysis.

Here are a couple instances in which analysis led to reports that led to action by the executive level/client of the organization:[1]

- A health care provider revamped a new-hire orientation program, with the goal of improving the retention rate of new hires. By looking at attrition rates for the period prior to the training redesign and then measuring the retention rates after the redesign for a few months, the provider found that the retention rates improved by 93%. The provider was also able to automate the measurement of the program to reduce measurement administration by 75%.

- A telecommunications equipment maker revamped its customer education program to be more hands-on and competency based. The unintended consequence was that the cost to manage the program doubled. The company needed credible metrics to overcome the cost increase, which was perceived as an expense rather than as an investment. Pilot participants' results were measured, and the metrics revealed an estimated 10% reduction in calls to the call center and a 12% reduction in error rates due to the training program. Overall, this was a cost savings for the company, which caused the training to be perceived as an investment rather than an expense.

The Most Critical Reporting and Analysis Practices

Respondents described seven general practices that are critical within reporting and analysis, as listed in Figure 9-1.

These practices are discussed further in the following sections.

Assess or Measure Learning Outcomes

High-performing training organizations measure and report on learning outcomes after the completion of training. Typically, outcomes are measured through some form of testing or demonstration of knowledge and skills. Ideally, training organizations should measure a learner's *changes* in knowledge and skills by "conducting assessments of learners' knowledge and skills before and after training events" as a director of training and development for a health care organization said.

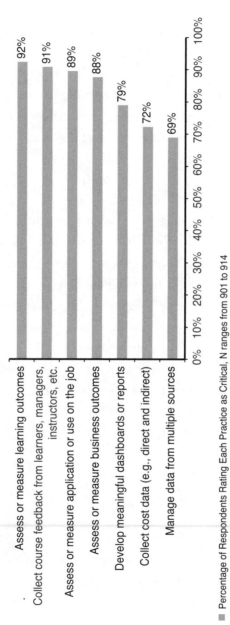

■ Percentage of Respondents Rating Each Practice as Critical, N ranges from 901 to 914

Figure 9-1   The Most Critical Reporting and Analysis Practices

Learning leaders and business executives are mutually interested in ensuring that training translates into improved business performance. Measuring the impact to the business is sometimes difficult when the training is more about communicating knowledge than about skills. For example, it is difficult to measure how leadership training changes the business because a manager's behavior improvements may not translate into immediate business improvement. Therefore, it's imperative to measure a student's level of knowledge before and after training to see what is retained and what is not.

Collect Feedback

High-performing training organizations recognize that information about how to improve the effectiveness of training comes from multiple sources. An organization should collect students' feedback about the quality of the training. In addition, it should collect results on managers and other stakeholders of the training to determine whether the students are carrying the learning from the classroom to the job. This practice is especially effective when done regarding professional skills, such as presentation skills, communication skills, team-building training, etc. Feedback can be as simple as informal interviews with the stakeholders of training to as formal as surveys and questionnaires to determine whether the training is making an impact to the business.

Assess or Measure Application on the Job

The truest measure of the effectiveness of training for the individual is to determine whether the learner has applied the skills to daily routines and tasks on the job. We have well covered the concept that training is not done for the sake of learning alone; it is done for the purpose of initiating specific actions or behaviors on the job. For employee training, specific on-the-job improvements and applications are expected and should be among the outcome metrics defined before the training. This type of evaluation (Level 3) is often accomplished through direct observation, using a technique such as time studies or job sampling to observe and score employees on how well they are applying their new knowledge or skills. It can also be done through indirect observation, using employee interviews, self-reported changes, or surveys.

A senior vice president for learning and performance solutions in a major financial institution provided an example of how a training organization was evaluated based on on-the-job performance: "We use a scorecard process to measure new-hire success once they transition to their teams. We are accountable for how well the new hire performs both in training and through their first 90 days on the job."

Assess or Measure Business Outcomes

The "Holy Grail" of measurement techniques is the ability to see how training actually impacts the bottom line of the business. With these Level 4 evaluations, we seek metrics that capture the impact of training, and then we convert those results into an ROI metric. Some consider measuring the impact of training through ROI the "ideal metric on key training initiatives," in the words of a corporate university training manager at a technology company. But while doing this may be ideal, most can appreciate that it is also very difficult.

ROI is a calculation: net benefits (i.e., benefits minus costs) divided by costs. The most difficult part of this equation is isolating and quantifying the benefit(s) of the training and controlling other variables that could impact the outcome metric. Even in areas like sales, where outcomes may be rather easily quantifiable, determining whether results are related to training or other factors can be problematic.

Note that while business outcome metrics can be used alone, other levels of evaluation, such as learning outcomes and on-the-job applications, can also help decipher training impact. Business impact is possible only if training occurs and learners then apply their new knowledge or skills on the job.

For instance, a consumer products company spent $5,000 per salesperson on sales training.[2] This was the most ever for this organization. The sales VP was interested in determining the ROI that the training created for the business. The company did a ROI analysis following the training, in which it attributed $74,000 in increased sales per salesperson to the sales training. This was a 14.8-fold return on the $5,000 investment, and this ability to measure the change helped the sales VP see the value in the training.

Develop Meaningful Dashboards or Reports

The use of learning dashboards requires training managers to define metrics and set goals so they can measure in real time, whether the organization is meeting or exceeding performance expectations. The purpose of learning dashboards is to provide management with real-time metrics that alert them to changes in the business—thus telling them when changes need to be made. They assist management in identifying issues as early as possible so they can deal with them proactively and keep the organization performing at a high level. Dashboards keep the key data visible—front and center. They allow leaders and operational staff to make adjustments quickly when processes get out of line. Speed is of the essence. The more relevant and concise the information, the faster and more accurate the decision making can be.

We want to be clear about the fact that dashboards do not provide the same value as monthly written reports or digital summaries of training results. Those reports and summaries are not timely, and oftentimes they come too late for anyone to make changes that would be needed to save thousands of dollars. Training dashboards align with corporate dashboards and focus on the right level of information, leaving out irrelevant or secondary data that can be distracting.

At a minimum, the key outcome metrics that are identified during strategic alignment and tested during reporting and analysis should be reported as the key indicators of a training program's performance.

For example, if your team delivered 20,000 hours of training to sales, partners, and support staff, is that a good metric?[3] Some CEOs and executive teams would see this as 10 labor-years lost in one reporting period. That is a volume metric, not a result metric. The result metric would be about the impact of those hours on the enterprise goals. An operational dashboard helps you decide what's important in managing a great organization. According to Chris Moore, founder of ZeroedIn, a workforce analytics consulting and platform company, there are many examples of good dashboard metrics, including aggregate cost, volume, and productivity metrics; supplier relationship metrics; and metrics on efficiency of backroom processes, effort and investment allocation, resource utilization, and effectiveness.

The biggest challenge in implementing dashboards is choosing the proper metrics to report on. According to Linda White, vice president of global performance and learning with Scotiabank, "Executives always want more information. But providing them the right information that helps them to manage the business is an ongoing challenge. Finding the metrics that most leaders in the business believe are key to managing the business is very hard." Scotiabank has had the most success by focusing on metrics like the type of training delivered as a percentage of mix—around areas such as compliance, sales, service, and leadership—and then comparing the mix of training to the bank's strategy to make sure the allocation of dollars and resources is in line with corporate objectives.

Collect Cost Data

As discussed previously, cost data is included in the ROI calculation. This includes both the direct costs of producing, administering, and delivering the training content and any travel or related expenses.

Cost data should incorporate indirect or opportunity cost, which takes into account the amount of time an employee spent in training instead of performing his or her job. This is why sometimes converting classroom training into elearning may have a higher upfront capital expenditure, but when calculating the total cost, including time away from the job, the savings may become apparent when there are large numbers of students to train. Collecting cost data fills an important basic need because when communicating with senior management, it allows for the development of a detailed discussion around returns on those investments.

Manage Data from Multiple Sources

Leaders of high-performing training organizations use financial data, information from the quality department, customer service data, client satisfaction data, and other lines of business to determine how training is impacting the business. The paradigm shift for many training managers is to recognize that only measuring the activities associated with their organization is not an indicator of success. The true indicator of success of high-performing training organizations is how activities impact the data of their client's organization.

Conclusion

This chapter addresses the importance of developing and tracking meaningful metrics associated with training outcomes and linking those metrics to measureable business outcomes. It also addresses the need to visibly communicate accurate and meaningful data in a timely and relevant manner to the stakeholders of training, including the learning leader, executive-level sponsor, and/or customer. Each of these data points is a fundamental driver for the analysis that drives future initiatives, including funding.

The seven best practices of reporting and analysis are:

- Assess or measure learning outcomes.
- Collect feedback.
- Assess or measure application on the job.
- Assess or measure business outcomes.
- Develop meaningful dashboards or reports.
- Collect cost data.
- Manage data from multiple sources.

The material covered in this chapter is a critical link to the discussion in Chapter 10, on portfolio management.

Notes

1. Berk, Jeffrey, "The Business Case for Measuring Learning," *Training Industry Quarterly*, Spring 2010, pp. 15–17.
2. Ibid.
3. Kelly, Tom, "My Training Dashboard? Which One?" *Training Industry Quarterly*, Fall 2012, pp. 27–29.

10

Portfolio Management

Portfolio management includes the ongoing selection and rationalization of formal training content, such as classroom and online courses, as well as informal content, such as books, documents, videos, and other knowledge-based assets that are a part of the training experience. Along with keeping learning curricula fresh and timely, the learning leader must ensure the curation of internal as well as externally aggregated content. The ability to manage large portfolios of learning content using organized and blended methodologies is instrumental to reducing costs and ensuring proper program positioning.

Portfolio management is very important in managing customer training programs. Courses need to be available when the customers need them. And the portfolios are often product based or job role based. Having a broad range of training products is critical in customer training scenarios.

High-performing portfolio management practices involves ensuring a diverse mix of titles, modalities, and levels of new versus tried-and-true courses. At Siemens, for instance, Norbert Neubauer, head of business development training, said, "In addition to innovative technologies and production processes, developing qualified employees and preparing them for advancement are crucial factors for any company's success. Our training helps our customers to optimally use our resources to develop an important competitive advantage."[1] The company offers more than 300 classroom courses at 200 locations in 60 countries, with more than 60,000 participants annually.

Neubauer tells us there are three good reasons Siemens maintains a portfolio of training programs:

- **Manufacturer expertise**—As the manufacturer of the products, Siemens starts developing the training during the product development stage so the training can be launched in parallel with the launch of the new product.

- **Practical relevance**—Courses at Siemens are recognized for their wide range of practical exercises, which usually account for half of the course time. This approach allows the learner to apply the knowledge immediately back on the job.

- **Flexible implementation**—Neubauer has said that flexibility is the name of the game. The content as well as the location of the training can be customized to meet each customer's needs.

You can get an initial sense of a training organization's portfolio management capabilities by simply browsing through its course catalog. How many different types of courses, with which methodologies, does the training organization offer? What instructional levels are offered? How many new courses are available? Are any courses outdated?

Understanding portfolio management capabilities at a deeper level may require an assessment of how well the training offerings are tied to "strategic business values"—as a senior manager of a corporate university in a technology firm noted. He added, "Remember not to lose focus on the client/customer." Simply having a broad offering of titles that has nothing to do with businesses objectives is not helpful and can be very costly.

An instructional designer at a training company reminded us of the connection between portfolio management and other capabilities that focus on aligning individual course content with strategic needs. The designer emphasized that portfolio management should "tie in with assessments, job analysis and other HR functions."

Getting the Portfolio Mix Right

What factors are the most important in making decisions about what training should be included in a portfolio? And how would you use these factors to evaluate whether your current portfolio has the right programs? These are important business questions that involve funding and resource allocation.[2]

Proper use of instructional systems design (ISD) methodologies can guide effective instructional design based on the needs of the business. Most often, ISD assumes that a business decision has already been made that training is needed. However, often a training manager assumes or takes over the responsibility of managing a training organization and needs to evaluate whether the training currently offered is the right training, aligned to the business's needs. In this situation, the learning leader or portfolio manager takes on the task of portfolio rationalization.

Portfolio rationalization is an exercise for evaluating courses within a training curriculum to determine which ones are useful and valued by the business and which ones are not. The ultimate objective is to determine whether courses or programs should be continued or eliminated. Criteria used to evaluate courses are generally related to strategic importance of the information, level of proprietary content contained within the course, alignment to business strategy, etc. Training Industry, Inc., teaches the use of the Portfolio Rationalization Four Quadrant Model as shown in Figure 10-1. This type of tool helps in evaluating a portfolio's usefulness. It is important to note that the portfolio rationalization exercise is not an evaluation for measuring or determining the quality of instructional design but rather one to determine a course's alignment to the business strategy.[3]

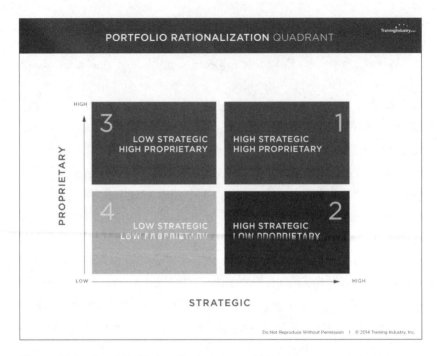

Figure 10-1   Portfolio Rationalization

All learning leaders must remember that the quality of a portfolio—meaning the effectiveness of the training, as measured by how well the business performs as a result of the training—strongly influences how the organization is perceived. If one or more courses are not right for the business, the organization will be viewed as missing the mark. Think about it from the standpoint of a retail store. When a consumer enters a store, looking for a particular good, and cannot find what he or she is looking for, the consumer may perceive that the store is not good because the product was not available. Effective portfolio management is an indicator to the learner of how well attuned the learning leader is to the needs of the business and how effective the learning leader is in making sure the right training is available when it is needed.

We have discussed in detail in this book the learning leader's challenge to create training that is directly aligned to the business and is done as a targeted investment of dollars related to a specific initiative.

But oftentimes a company must create an inventory or a library of courses that are available to the learner when the learner needs it. This can be an incredibly effective strategy for organizations where there are very large numbers of learners who need access to relevant, how-to information when they need it. Sometimes this content is not considered mission critical, but it is vitally important to learners when they need it. Installers provide a great example of the need for supply-driven content. When telecom equipment installers are in the field or on a customer site and encounter a problem, they can't stop the installation and wait two months for an available course to teach them how to deal with the problem. They need to learn immediately how to solve that problem and complete the installation to make sure the customer is satisfied.

Performance support systems are great examples of portfolios of learning content that are available on demand to the learner, when the learner needs it, and accessible in the modality that is best for a particular situation. Remember from Chapter 5 that Microsoft delivers training to software engineers by using a blended model called Learning Paths. Learning Paths is a great example of a portfolio of learning titles directly aligned to the needs of the learner and available when and where the learner needs it.

Learning portfolios are a published list of available titles and programs. Therefore, having content available in a way that is best for the learner to consume it is important. Determining the best way for a learner to access content is important in selecting the type of delivery mechanism that works best. For example, if call center employees are all home based and dispersed through many geographic locations, having a portfolio of courses that are all classroom based doesn't make sense for the audience. On the other hand, if your objective is to keep the sales force in the field as much as possible, having on-demand, online training is a good idea because it enables the learner to access content when needed, even on the road.

Training in an organization should come in many forms and should be accessed and delivered using various strategies. Content that is considered conceptual knowledge generally has a long shelf life and is needed by a large audience; this content can often be put online and made available in an on-demand format. Examples of this type of content include courseware and informal information for onboarding new employees and information on meeting compliance requirements for certification.

Content that is considered procedural knowledge is generally dynamic and needs to be updated frequently or is needed by a small audience; this type of content is best delivered to the audience that needs it at the time it is needed. Each of these examples represents content that is managed in a portfolio of offerings but accessed and delivered in very different ways. The challenge for a leader of a training organization is to determine during the content development cycle how to deliver or allow access to the material in the most economical way.

The Most Critical Portfolio Management Practices

Of the eight capability areas necessary for a great training organization, respondents in our study viewed portfolio management as the least important. This doesn't mean that it is not important, but it does say that leaders of high-performing training organizations understand that the supply of training, or libraries of content, is less critical than the need for targeted, mission-critical training directly tied to the company's objectives.

Our study identified five portfolio management practices, three of which respondents rated significantly higher than the others (see Figure 10-2). In terms of content offerings, these results depict the value that respondents place on new and updated material, as well as content depth instead of topic breadth. The following sections examine these five practices.

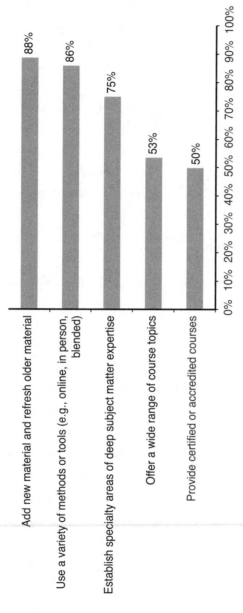

■ Percentage of Respondents Rating Each Practice as Critical, N ranges from 902 to 911

Figure 10-2   The Most Critical Portfolio Management Practices

Add New Material and Refresh Older Material

One of the most valuable ways for a training organization to increase its impact is to ensure that content remains current and fresh, based on changes in the business. The business never stands still, so training materials related to the business must constantly be added, and older content must be modified to stay up to date. Adding and updating content require structured feedback loops between the instructors and students' evaluations, which let a portfolio manager know where changes are required. In addition, frequent reviews by subject matter experts ensure that course materials are in line with current practices. Content that has a high orientation to technology will generally need more frequent refreshment, whereas nontechnical training (e.g., related to interpersonal communications skills) may continue to be as relevant today as it was five years ago.

To keep content current, some respondents told us the focus should be on the process. An associate director of learning design and development of a large financial services firm said that training organizations should create a "well-defined content maintenance process." The manager of operations and systems training of a tobacco company shared this thought: "Training documents are maintained electronically as controlled documents which require an annual review. This ensures documents are continuously reviewed and updated. Every updated or new procedure is documented and training delivered to employees, then the material is updated in the manuals."

Other companies focus on *which people* to involve in decisions to keep portfolio offerings current. The director of training and development for an accounting firm said that business owners should be involved, particularly in "decisions regarding prioritization and funding of projects in the portfolio—[since] the pie just doesn't get bigger as needs grow."

Use a Variety of Methods or Tools

Not all learners learn the same way. Moreover, not all learners are available to take courses at the same time. These two facts alone require training organizations to make their content available in a variety of ways (e.g., online, in person, blended). As the owner of a training consulting firm advised, "Enable learners to learn in the way that is most effective for the learner."

Training organizations should also evaluate their instructors when they review their programs' delivery capabilities. A program manager in a major telecommunications firm said, "Periodically evaluate the quality of the program, including facilitators of instructor-led training."

As for which methods should be used, a director of strategy and organizational development at a university said that it is important for training organizations to "have online learning capabilities" in addition to instructor-led or face-to-face courses. Similarly, a learning leader at a professional services firm said that "multiple methods to learning core skills and competencies" are present in great training organizations.

Mark Bower, the founder of Edge Interactive, points to the cornucopia of new possibilities for learning portfolios, and he says it's not just technology for technology's sake. Given the fast pace of business, the reduced number of managers and increased number of individuals reporting to each manager, and the endless flow of emails and other daily distractions, he has said that there "is not time to develop a skilled workforce using traditional methods."[4] Computer-based training as part of a broader-based portfolio both spans geographic distances and lets learners access and learn on their own schedules. The following are just some of the new portfolio learning solution choices:

- Instructor-led virtual classroom training
- Self-paced elearning
- Mobile learning
- Performance support and context-driven learning
- Blogs, wikis, and online communities
- Online resources and self-directed searches

Establish Specialty Areas of Deep Subject Matter Expertise

To ensure that training content is relevant to the learner's job or specific needs, portfolios must be organized in a way that keeps relevant content easily accessible and communicated in a way that addresses recommended order or pathways. The antithesis of this is producing a portfolio of training programs organized in alphabetical order. With such a system, the course titles may be easy to find, but the learner can't easily see which ones are relevant, and which ones are recommended before the others. Learners need and expect all the relevant information to be available for them to find easily and understandably. If the learner only gets titles of content and must search for more information after the training experience to determine what is important, the portfolio loses relevance and cost-effectiveness. It's important to design portfolios around jobs, topics, or initiatives rather than just organize around topics. Remember the example of Learning Paths with Microsoft. A manager for corporate learning and development at a Fortune 500 technology corporation emphasized that training organizations should have a "focused curriculum" and not be "all things to all people." More focused providers set themselves apart from those who seek to be jacks of all trades. Such organizations can benefit from knowing their strengths, sticking to them, and sourcing additional needs that clients may have.

Offer a Wide Range of Course Topics

Although a large percentage of respondents view established areas of expertise as critical, some clients prefer the one-stop convenience of viewing and selecting a wide range of topics from one provider. In praising a supplier's courseware library, one training leader of an insurance company valued being able to "find what I want when I want it."

Having a wide range of topics may not apply only to content areas but also to the types of employees for whom the training is designed. One manager of professional development at a company in the energy industry prefers that training organizations "offer development programs across the company—not just for managers or senior management."

Provide Certified or Accredited Courses

Knowing that training offerings have been vetted and validated by third-party sources, especially the originating source of the intelligence, creates confidence and credibility in the learner. Although our study found that this practice is considered less important than the other practices of high-performing training organizations, almost half of the respondents still feel that it is an important practice in managing an organization. For example, companies with a high orientation to technology, such as those in the software and health care fields, require that training provided to employees be licensed content from the source of the content. Some IT organizations only recognize training that is "licensed" or "certified" from the technology company it relates to, such as Microsoft or Cisco. As another example, ongoing training for nurses and medical staff is accredited by an industry-recognized association. Continuing medical education must be accredited by licensed providers. This is so important in the medical field that an organization called the Accreditation Council for Continuing Medical Education ensures that all training developed and delivered follows the rigor necessary for quality training.

Conclusion

Portfolio management involves the ongoing selection and rationalization of formal training content, such as classroom and online courses, as well as informal content, such as books, documents, videos, and other knowledge assets that are part of the training experience. Portfolio management is very important in managing customer training programs.

The quality of a portfolio influences perceptions of the quality of the organization. This chapter explores how to get the portfolio mix right and why it's necessary that a company creates an inventory, or a library of courses that are available to the learner when the learner needs it. This chapter also looks at why you need to keep modalities in mind when managing a portfolio, as well as the advantages of online learning libraries.

This chapter examines five best practices for portfolio management:

- Add new material or refresh older materials.
- Use a variety of methods or tools.
- Establish specialty areas with deep subject matter expertise.
- Offer a wide range of course topics.
- Provide certified or accredited courses.

Chapter 11 focuses on the role of technology in learning.

Notes

1. Siemens, "Well-Founded, First-Hand Knowledge," www. industry.siemens.com/services/global/en/portfolio/training/ Pages/index.aspx.

2. Harward, Doug, "Portfolio Rationalization Quadrant: What Training Do We Offer? What Do We Cut?" *Training Industry*, 2009, www.trainingindustry.com/articles/portfolio-rationalization-quadrant-what-training-do-we-offer-what-do-you-cut.aspx.

3. TrainingIndustry.com, "Portfolio Rationalization," www. trainingindustry.com/taxonomy/p/portfolio-rationalization. aspx.

4. Bower, Mark, "Instructional Design: Learning Meets Technology," *Training Industry Quarterly*, Fall 2011.

11

The Role of Technology in Learning

There is no question that the classroom is no longer what it used to be. Technologies have expanded the four walls of the classroom to a virtual learning world. With the ongoing innovation of technologies for learning, the trend is to allow students more flexibility to learn about what they want to learn about, when they want to learn about it, how they want to learn about it, from just about any place they choose.

The early days of using technology in corporate training focused on administration and content delivery. The learning management system (LMS) was an early innovation created to help a manager track and measure how much training was being delivered, so the manager would know where the money was being spent and who was taking and completing training. At the same time, consumer-oriented technologies were being brought into the classroom to assist facilitators in making content more interesting and engaging. The use of video and projection systems allowed instructors to make content more engaging and visible.

We quickly moved to a world of online training, where elearning became an approach that many believed would revolutionize learning. Although in theory it made sense during the early days of computing technology, it wasn't until the introduction of the Internet that elearning became economically feasible to the masses.

When we reflect on these early days of innovation in training, we see that technology was initially focused on making training more efficient. Training has always been viewed as a cost of doing business, and folks saw that if technology could help minimize some part of the cost of training, especially when large numbers of people needed to be trained, then it could be an effective investment.

The role of technology in learning has evolved from cost savings to today's greater focus on effectiveness. The focus is now much more on access to information, to other learners, and to relevant content, with the expectation that all this access will translate into faster behavior transformation.

We can now say that the single biggest revolutionary technology to impact the training market in the past 30 years has been the search engine. It has exponentially increased our access to knowledge-based content—as well as any other type of information we can imagine. The ability to get fast access to information that can help us solve a problem, learn how to do something, or just get information about where something is located is literally at our fingertips. Learner's can go online and get a solution to a business problem in literally seconds. No longer does a learner have to wait several weeks or months to take a class to get an answer about how to solve a problem. As efficient as all this may seem, it has also created challenges for training professionals.

Because information is so readily available, the need to memorize or even learn information is less required now than it ever has been. Betsy Sparrow at Columbia University, Jenny Liu at University of Wisconsin, and Daniel Wegner at Harvard University dubbed this phenomenon the "Google Effect" in their 2011 research study.[1] They found that learners who have easy access to the Internet are less likely to remember information that is easily accessible online.

Training professionals must recognize the Google Effect and its influence on their students. Search engine technologies have changed not only how we learn but how we behave in every walk of life. Training professionals must be conscious of the fact that learners are becoming much more independent in how they get information, and they're becoming less dependent on facilitators or training providers. This means training professionals must think very differently about how they design content for consumption—and how they make it available.

For example, learners often access information on mobile devices, but those devices are not designed for long-term access. Learners use mobile devices for short-term data gathering, and then they move on to other activities. To reach users on mobile devices, content must be designed to be accessed as shorter, consumable objects. Think of the explosion of how-to videos on YouTube, the single largest portal of how-to information in the world. A recent search on YouTube for "How To" got more than 270 million results. Many corporations are choosing YouTube as a platform for hosting their customer training videos. The challenge for training professionals is to make sure the content learners go to at YouTube, or Wikipedia, or Google is relevant to the jobs they are doing. This is the fundamental issue that we now confront, and it is the challenge we as training professionals must embrace.

Leaders of high-performing training organizations are embracing various technologies. Employees of chain restaurants like the Cheesecake Factory have YouTube-like learning portals for sharing how to do a particular task well, whether cleaning a floor or preparing a meal. Employees have also begun creating cell phone videos in a viral and interactive way to share the right ways to do some tasks as well as humorous stories about how they solved problems on the job.[2]

Consider the advantage of pilots learning on flight simulators before they actually take to the air and put their lives and expensive equipment at risk. For instance, Boeing released its newest incarnation of its 777 jet in 2013, and a small company called Precision

Manuals Development Group LLC released the 777 version of its flight simulator software shortly after that. The software replicates in exact and realistic detail every facet of flying the long-range jetliner. Learners can experience the exact handling characteristics of the 777, including hearing the custom sounds of every knob and switch. The software costs under $100 per pilot, while the cost of a 777 is $296 million.[3]

Technology-based training makes available a wide array of data, information, videos, lectures, and discussion groups to the learner. It requires the training leader to go beyond the unmandated source of content (i.e., search engine) to the kind of organizational-specific information that the training organization can mandate and curate and make available through proprietary and protected repositories. These repositories, referred to as *knowledge repositories*, and previously referred to as libraries of content, are online databases that systematically capture, organize, and categorize knowledge-based information into an easy-to-use and easy-to-access format. Knowledge repositories are most often private databases that manage enterprise and proprietary information, although public repositories also exist to manage public domain intelligence related to customer training needs.

For example, companies like Cisco and IBM provide online environments where customers can access product information at any time. Oftentimes these environments charge for certain types of information because of the sensitivity of intellectual information. Sometimes a company makes this information available for free because it wants more prospective customers to have access to its materials. Some companies that have very sensitive information and want to protect the distribution and use of intelligence in the public domain are choosing digital rights management. This is a class of technologies that control copying, printing, and alteration of works. These types of repositories are often plug-ins to corporate websites, with many security and analytics features included.

Technologies Should Enable the Learning Experience and Never Be a Distraction

The effective use of technology by great training organizations focuses on enhancing how a learner consumes content and interfaces with administrators, facilitators, and other learners. Technology should not be cumbersome, difficult to navigate, or intermittent in performance. If it is, it has the potential to be a distraction and get in the way of the learning experience.

Learners today are choosing to bring their own device to the learning experience—whether it be in the formal classroom, or to informal access of learning information. This concept has been phrased BYOD, or "Bring Your Own Device." The challenge for training organizations is to embrace the idea that learners have many choices about what type of device they will access content with, and make sure the content fits any device. This is important in making sure that the technology doesn't look like a distraction to the learner.

A few short years ago, many viewed Second Life as a promising tool for corporate training. Second Life is a three-dimensional virtual world whose content is open-ended and created by its users, based on their imagination. Despite Second Life's potential for simulated training and education, many teachers and trainers found it to be good for interaction but weak on document storage and grade book functions. In addition to its limited utility for instruction, its poor security and lack of marketing utility prompted organizations such as Wells Fargo and Starwood Hotels and Resorts to leave Second Life and pursue alternative simulation environments. The issue was that it was possible for learners to violate an organization's virtual world guidelines, which hampered corporate trainers and university instructors to control and maintain their learning environments.[4]

This doesn't mean Second Life is or was a bad simulation world. It's quite good at what it is designed to do. But as a training environment, its very creativeness and openness provides too much leeway for some trainees to wander from the desired learning path and not stay focused on the intent of the learning design.

Match Tools to Learning Styles

It is no secret that everyone learns differently. Some consider themselves visual learners, others auditory. Some believe that the age of the learner dictates the design and delivery strategy for the content being delivered. The challenge for training leaders is to recognize that learning is a process and not a product. Using technologies for training is about creating an environment between the learner and the content that allows for the consumption of information to be experiential, letting learners examine and test ideas and then integrate them into their daily jobs. A good approach is to first understand the learners and then choose the most appropriate technologies. Companies all too often get caught up in technology trends and try to make learners adapt to tools. Great training organizations focus on understanding the needs of learners and choosing tools that meet those styles.

Technologies Can Reduce the Barriers of Geography and Time

Many learning leaders are responsible for delivering training to learners all over the world and then making sure the content is delivered consistently and in a timely manner that respects the cultural and geographic needs of the learners. Distributing content to global audiences was traditionally very time-consuming, as materials had to be shipped to every location and then facilitators had to be prepped on how to deliver the materials to local audiences. Virtual learning technologies now allow training to be delivered simultaneously to many locations around the world, with learners in all regions receiving the same training at the same time. Virtual learning technologies are essential when support groups such as call centers are located in remote countries and need to be trained on what clients need to know in other locations. High-performing training organizations utilize virtual technologies to speed the time to delivery of content to global audiences.

Technology Standards Allow for Improved Interoperability and Access of Content

In the early 1990s, there was a growing need to make sure online training could be accessed and delivered consistently via any learning content management system (LCMS). As the popularity of elearning content grew, and more organizations began creating online courseware, creative approaches to design meant that all LCMSs could not support all content. To resolve this issue, the U.S. Department of Defense (DoD) created an effort called the Advanced Distributed Learning (ADL) initiative, with a comprehensive strategy to integrate learning content and technologies and transition department-wide training efforts. Specifically, the ADL initiative was meant to provide "a network of dispersed accessible and reusable learning content by creating a set of standardized guidelines for the implementation and use of technology in learning." Through research and guidance on technological challenges related to distributed learning, the objective was to create cost-effective technology-based learning systems capable of generating profits for industry and a forum for partners to exchange knowledge of distance learning on a large scale. To make everything compatible, the ADL initiative produced the Sharable Content Object Reference Model (SCORM). The DoD asserts that

SCORM facilitates the creation of reusable content as "instructional objects" within a common technical framework. LMSs that conform to SCORM standards are more readily able to interact with content utilized in other management systems.

In the past couple years, the ADL initiative has created a second set of standards, called the Tin Can API, or also referred to as the Experience API (xAPI). Often referred to as the next generation of SCORM, these standards are an open source application programming interface (API) created to address a few drawbacks of SCORM by providing several new capabilities, such as more control over learning content, the ability to track real-world performance, and the ability to track learning plans and goals. Whereas SCORM was created to allow multiple LMSs to interact with multiple forms of elearning, Tin Can was formed to create a more measurable approach to managing informal content.

Conclusion

This chapter examines the role of technology in learning and important considerations for how to maximize the effectiveness of the use of technologies. It also looks at how technologies enable learning but can also distract users from learning. Technology can help drive goals such as consistency for global programs, and it can solve time and location issues. Technology has altered training in terms of:

- Cost
- Efficiency
- Effectiveness

Chapter 12 takes a look at how technology is integrated into an organization's training program.

Notes

1. Betsy Sparrow, *et al.*, "Google Effects on Memory: Cognitive Consequences of Having Information at Our Fingertips," *Science* **333**:6043:776-778 doi:10.1126/science.1207745, July 15, 2011.

2. Bersin, Josh, "5 Keys to Building a Learning Organization," *Forbes*, January 18, 2012. www.forbes.com/sites/joshbersin/2012/01/18/5-keys-to-building-a-learning-organization/.

3. http://www.precisionmanuals.com/ProductCart/pc/view Categories.asp?idCategory=13

4. Taylor, Kevin, and Seung Youn Chyung, "Would You Adopt Second Life as a Training and Development Tool?" *Performance Improvement*, Vol. 47, No. 8, September 2008.

12

Technology Integration

Learners are inundated with ways to get access to knowledge—attending classes, reading books, watching videos, taking elearning courses, searching for answers via the Internet, and participating in online games, chat rooms, social media sites—the list goes on and on. There are so many ways to learn through technology, it's a challenge for a training manager to understand which tool is most effective and when it works best. Where should leaders of training organizations spend company money? What is the best way to integrate all the various forms of technologies to create a seamless learning experience?

High-performing training organizations utilize the vast array of technologies available to them in an integrated and effective way. They don't just use technology for technology's sake or because it's cool and enhances the training experience. There must be a strategy for how to leverage the technologies available to a learner—and to a business—in a way that impacts and transforms the learner's behavior. Proper integration of technology allows the learner to get the information needed when it's needed. In addition, integration allows a training manager to deliver information they need to deliver, when they need to deliver it, to the people who most need to receive it. And it allows managers to measure and analyze the consumption of information in a way that helps drive the next generation of information consumption and dissemination.

For a training manager, the use of technology is about the cost-effectiveness of training; it's about strategically aligning the right training to drive business performance.

Technology Platforms

To understand how to integrate technologies, let's first explore the various types of technology platforms and how to use them in the training experience:

- **Administrative platform**—The most-used learning technology in the corporate setting is the administrative platform. Most commonly referred to as learning management systems (LMSs), administrative platforms assist in managing the back-office tasks related to tracking activities and automating communications between an administrator, trainer/instructor, and learner. There are many generations of administrative platforms, with varying degrees of sophistication, including the LMS, the learning content management system (LCMS), the learning portal, and now the personal learning environment. Each of them provides an administrative system that brings together all the constituents of the training process. Included in the discussion of administration technologies are tools such as knowledge repositories, analytics, ecommerce, and search.

- **Authoring platform**—Another technology platform that has gained traction over the years is the authoring platform. Authoring tools allows trained instructional designers to create sophisticated online training programs, and they also allow novice designers and subject matter experts (SMEs) to convert standard presentation materials into online courses. Authoring tools allow an instructional designer or SME to focus on good instructional design without having to be an expert in software design. It simplifies the process of putting content into an online environment. The vast array of authoring platforms originally assisted instructional designers in using the ADDIE process (Analysis, Design, Develop, Implementation, Evaluation) and have now evolved to helping novice designers—typically SMEs—convert standard content such as PowerPoint files into online elearning courses. This requires simply uploading a PowerPoint file, recording voice (audio) over the file, embedding a video, and adding test or evaluation questions at the end of the course.

- **Delivery platform**—The third technology that is an important toolset for the training manager is the delivery platform. Early day delivery platforms provided a means for learners to have access to an elearning course, to have it tracked and integrated with the admin platform (LMS), and to play it on a ubiquitous computing device. Today's delivery tools go well beyond that to where they provide for virtual delivery of content in a formal training setting, to the delivery of content in informal environments, such as remote labs, conference rooms, on a mobile device and more,

- **Collaboration platform**—The most recent addition to the learning technology family is the collaboration platform. Also known as social learning tools, these environments provide a learner the ability to easily communicate and share information with other learners and the facilitator — before, during, and after the learning experience or outside the formal classroom.

In today's high-tech world, most training now involves the use of technology and the integration of learning-related tools with enterprise software applications. Whether a student is accessing content via an LMS, playing or viewing a course remotely, or communicating with other learners when assistance is needed, the integration of training systems with enterprise systems is more important than ever before. It involves the ability to integrate those technologies with other supply chain or talent management systems—including succession planning, recruiting, performance management, and compensation as well as learning—and enterprise resource planning (ERP) systems. To effectively integrate with these enterprise wide systems, training organizations must communicate effectively with both internal IT staff and the IT teams of partners and suppliers.

Successful integration improves efficiency and enables better measurement of and reporting on the impact of training. It can also eliminate the need for duplicate data entry and maintenance. The frequency with which information is shared, or integrated, between systems can range from real time to daily, weekly, monthly, or not at all.

Technology Is an Enabler of Engagement and Good Measurement

When technologies are properly integrated, they can greatly enable or facilitate learner engagement and allow for much more effective measurement of the learning experience. Although we often think of technology integration between the various platforms, the bigger challenge is how to link content with technology to create a truly balanced and positive experience for the learner. This level of integration allows for improved accessibility, flexibility, and scalability. Our research has identified several ideas about how technology can assist with learner engagement and measurement:

- Interaction with instructors and peers can be important to learner satisfaction and can provide reinforcement of the learning objective (i.e., that learners need to gain competency). This interaction can be achieved electronically using synchronous means, but traditional face-to-face meetings might be preferred. Thus, blended learning strategies still have a place in good interaction.

- Just reading content on a computer screen is not good interaction. Trainees need active engagement, opportunities for discovery learning, peer interactive discussions and activities, and chances to apply what they have learned. For this reason, interactive multimedia programs result in better comprehension, increased retention, and effective transfer of skills and knowledge.

- Trainees also agree that the content must be relevant, timely, and connected to the things they already know.

- Measurement and feedback help support trainees during the training experience. When trainees make mistakes, they need to know as soon as possible so they can learn how to avoid the same mistakes the next time. Interpersonal interaction is vital to both the trainee and the training administrator.

The Most Critical Technology Integration Practices

In our study, more than two-thirds of training professionals felt the five technology integration practices were critical (see Figure 12-1). The five practices are discussed in the following sections.

Use Consultative Skills to Develop an Integration Plan

In technology integration, all training organizations need strong consultative skills in order to navigate the complex and diverse array of technology platforms. While a training organization may lack the technical know-how to get systems integrated, 76% of respondents expect that they have the skills to at least consult with the right technical people to identify integration requirements and create an appropriate integration plan. The role of a training manager is not to be a technical expert in how to do the integration but to provide consultative support in determining the requirements for integration, to define what the expected user experience should be after integration, to develop policies and practices for how information should be input into the systems, and to develop policies and practices for how information will be extracted and mined from the system.

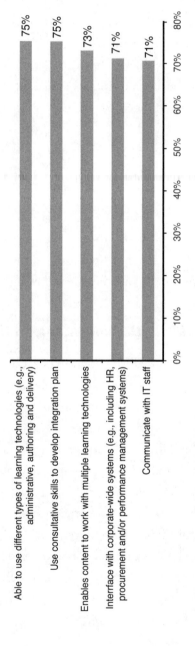

■ Percentage of Respondents Rating Each Practice as Critical, N ranges from 903 to 907

Figure 12-1 The Most Critical Technology Integration Practices

Able to Use Different Types of Learning Technologies

High-performing training organizations demonstrate the ability to use a variety of different learning technologies, and they do so in a way that successfully impacts the learning experience. According to a learning designer in the health care industry, "It is critical to an organization's training function to fully understand the technology of their systems."

Emerging Technologies

With which types of technologies should training organizations be familiar? Between 2010 and 2013, we asked respondents which technologies they use now or will be expected to use in the near future. Here's how they responded:

- Virtual instructor-led training (e.g., through audio, web, and video conferencing)
- Rapid elearning tools (e.g., PowerPoint conversion tools)
- Learning portals where learners can find and access many learning resources (including many of the other technologies listed)
- Company-generated knowledge management/performance support/reference tools
- Immersive learning (e.g., simulations, games, virtual worlds)
- Social, user-generated tools (e.g., social media, Web 2.0, wikis, blogs, communities of practice)
- Podcasting (i.e., audio or video files released episodically)
- Mobile devices (e.g., tablets, smart phones)

Figure 12-2 shows the emerging learning technologies reportedly used most often from 2010 to 2012, in order from most to least used. By far the most commonly used technology is virtual instructor-led training. It was interesting the degree of adoption we found in the use of the newer technologies. Of note about 60% of organizations use learning portals and rapid elearning tools and 50% use company knowledge management or reference tools.

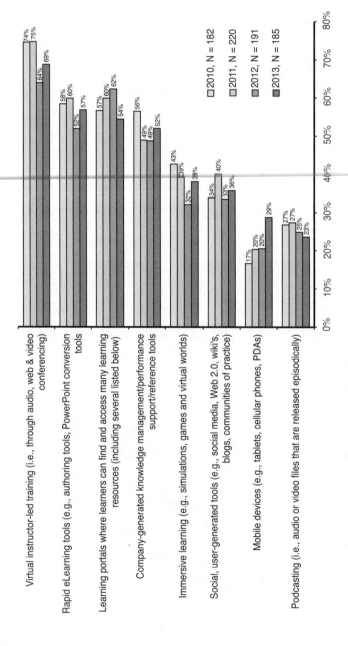

Figure 12-2 Actual Use of Emerging Learning Technologies

Expected Use of Emerging Learning Technologies, 2010–2012

Leaders of training organizations were asked which learning technologies have been growing fastest in their enterprise. The top four technologies listed—virtual instructor-led training, rapid elearning tools, learning portals where learners can find and access many learning resources, and company-generated knowledge management/performance support/reference tools—were used by 50% or more of respondents. Of these four technologies, learning portals and company knowledge management or reference tools adoption is expected to grow the most—with the largest percentages of individuals and companies expecting to use these technologies. Among the less-used technologies, mobile devices are growing the fastest (see Figure 12-3), closely followed by social, user-generated tools and podcasting. Figure 12-3 illustrates these growth figures, in order of highest to lowest expected use rate over the three-year period.

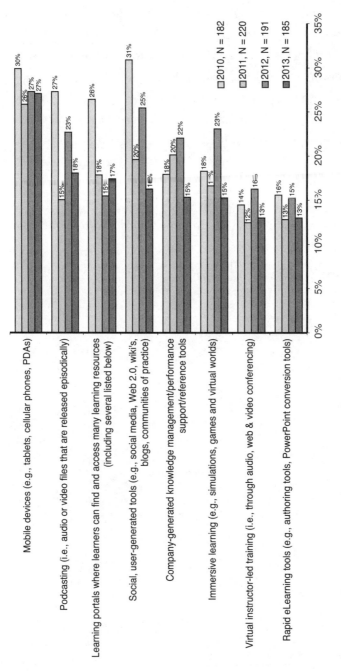

Figure 12-3   Expected Use of Emerging Learning Technologies

Enables Content to Work with Multiple Learning Technologies

Different lines of business or groups within a company have varying preferences for learning tools; some are comfortable with tools that are easy to use, while others want learning tools that will save time and create efficiencies. Since more training *content* is being shared than ever before, training organizations must know how to format or otherwise integrate content into the delivery platforms. This includes integrating content across various devices, computer environments, and management systems. High-performing training organizations should be able to design content that is impartial to specific tools but that leverages the benefits of each particular technology (e.g., chat rooms). The challenge here is that learning leaders are responsible for understanding the needs of the business and ensuring that training meets those needs. In doing that, they have to recognize that all learners have different preferences about how they like to learn. All enterprises have learners from various age groups, different personality styles, and cultural differences; also, importantly, they have many different technologies available to access training. Learning leaders must design content that allows learners to bring their own devices to the training experience, and the content needs to recognize each device and configure it in a way that allows the content to conform to the device—not make a learner compromise his or her learning style.

Interface with Corporate-wide Systems

Training technologies do not exist within a training department vacuum—they are part of an intricate network of an enterprise's IT environment. In fact, they are somewhat ubiquitous to other technologies used for other purposes. Delivery platforms are often part of the environment used for meeting and virtual conference events. For example, frequently used virtual meeting platforms such as WebEx or GotoMeeting, are also used for internal training events.

Learning leaders of high-performing training organizations recognize that the interaction between learning technologies and critical corporate systems requires careful planning. Corporate-wide systems include financial systems (where internal costs of training may need to be cross charged as a cost allocation requirement), ERP systems (where employee records must be integrated with their training transcripts), forecasting tools (where planned training expenditures must be integrated with financial budgets), and manufacturing systems (where compliance data must be integrated with training completion records). Learning technologies may extract data from these systems and should follow the same data entry, privacy, and maintenance rules as the company's other systems.

Communicates with IT Staff

Approximately 70% of the respondents in our study said they believe that great training organizations should have excellent communicators who can understand information technology well enough to exchange technical requirements with IT staff. Oftentimes, IT and other departments look to learning leaders for training leadership and support.

An instructional designer in a home health care company told us that training organizations should not only communicate with IT staff but should "make them an integral part of the analysis stage to understand the limitations and capabilities of the organization's system platforms."

When Marriott switched from Windows XP and Office 2003 to Windows 7 and Office 2010, the impact was felt on 60,000 computers and about 100,000 employees throughout the Marriott network.[1] The training staff had to partner with the internal IT organization, as well as external training suppliers, to make the transition. John K. Hart, the director of IT learning solutions and enterprise desktop training at Marriott, said, "The most important thing to do is to minimize the disruption. A quiet turnover is a successful turnover."

Jule Baradi, senior director of learning governance at Marriott, explained, "In the area of technology, we don't have the time and luxury for building custom products. We want to keep up with what's happening in the marketplace, so we heavily leverage external experts that can help us get things out the door quickly."

In this case, Marriott utilized Element K, a SkillSoft company, to create elearning courses and job aids. Because Marriott employees didn't have time to take entire courses, the company asked Element K to repackage and repurpose existing elearning course materials into more bite-sized content.

Marriott worked with Custom Guide to explore a library of checklists and cheat sheets and to license an acquired set of resources on the corporate intranet site, tailored to Marriott's own ways and needs.

By learning approaches used by other training organizations and leveraging vendor products, Marriott successfully created a self-service atmosphere where employees felt comfortable and able to learn at their own pace, in their own time.

Conclusion

This chapter looks at what good technology integration is, how it can be achieved by partnering with internal IT and service providers, and how it can enable engagement and good measurement.

This chapter also looks at how good integration works as well as how a great program can be impacted by poor integration. There are five best practices of technology integration:

- Able to use different types of learning technologies.
- Use consultative skills to develop an integration plan.

- Enable your content to work with multiple learning technologies (including a look at emerging technologies).

- Interface with corporate-wide systems such as HR, Procurement, ERP, sales force data, and financial systems.

- Communicate well with the IT staff.

This wraps up the tour of basic concepts and best practices necessary to making yours a high-performing organization that is on its way to greatness. Chapter 13 provides a summary of all that the book has covered as well as the takeaways you can consider and use yourself

Note

1. Eggleston, Michelle, "Marriott: Accommodating IT Training," *Training Industry Quarterly*, Winter 2010, pp. 37–39.

13

Summary and Key Takeaways

Successful training professionals are constantly seeking ways to improve the effectiveness and efficiency of their training organizations—whether through the programs they offer or the processes for which they identify, develop, and deliver training. Our research has found that the best path to success is to focus on the processes associated with managing a training function and implementing a clear set of practices that make training a valuable component of the business. We sought to understand those practices better and embarked on what has now been a seven-year journey to better understand what makes a great training organization.

What we have found is that there are groups of processes, or practices, that we refer to as *capabilities*. We have also found that virtually all training organizations have some level of expertise in eight key capability areas, which we define in this book. Organizations that excel in many of the practices associated with each capability are thought to be performing at what we consider a *great* level. Some companies monetize these capabilities, and others employ them in running their own training organizations.

The Eight Process Capabilities

In our study, we asked learning leaders to rate which process capabilities have been most important to their success. In addition, we asked them to provide opinions on not only which processes are most important but also which ones help propel organizations from good to great. The study found eight capability areas across most training organizations, which Figure 13-1 shows ranked from most to least important.

For your reference, here we have included a brief definition of each capability area shown in Figure 13-1:

- **Strategic alignment**—Ability to design learning programs that align with business objectives.
- **Content development**—Assessment, design, management, and maintenance of content.
- **Delivery**—Ability to manage an instructor network and deliver training using multiple modalities.
- **Diagnostics**—Ability to identify causes of problems and make recommendations.
- **Reporting and analysis**—Ability to define business metrics and report data to make improvements.
- **Technology integration**—Ability to integrate learning technologies with other learning technologies or other corporate applications.
- **Administrative services**—Scheduling, registration, technology, and other support functions.
- **Portfolio management**—Ability to manage, rationalize, and maintain large portfolios of courses.

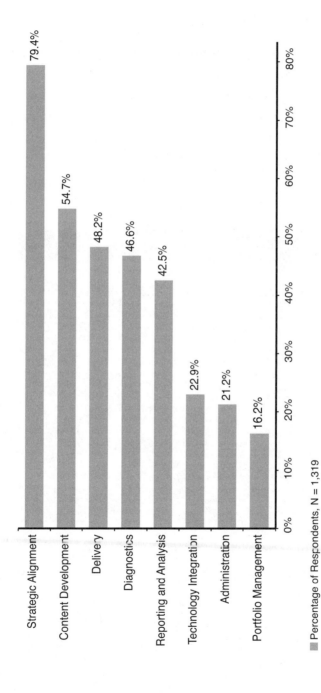

Strategic Alignment — 79.4%
Content Development — 54.7%
Delivery — 48.2%
Diagnostics — 46.6%
Reporting and Analysis — 42.5%
Technology Integration — 22.9%
Administration — 21.2%
Portfolio Management — 16.2%

Percentage of Respondents, N = 1,319

Figure 13-1   Process Capabilities

Practices for Each Process Capability Area

We have developed two reference charts that have become favorites of many learning leaders who have been involved or exposed to the findings of our research. The first, shown in Figure 13-2, shows the eight process capabilities and the key practices that learning leaders told us were most critical in each. In this chart, the process capabilities for building a great training organization are ranked from most to least critical, and the practices are also ranked from most to least critical.

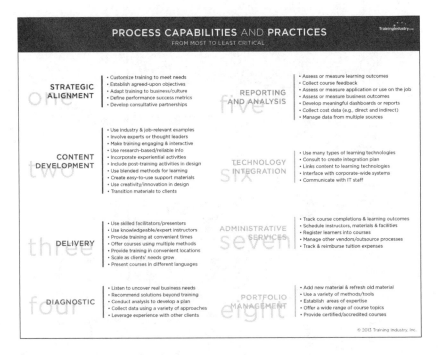

Figure 13-2   Process Capabilities and Practices

This chart provides a great reminder of what to focus on each day, with strategic alignment being the first consideration in beginning a program, task, or project.

Figure 13-3 places the same practices in sequence, from most to least critical, regardless of the capability areas in which they fall. This chart is particularly helpful for getting focused on first things first. The number next to each practice is the percentage of learning leaders in our study who felt that the practice is critical. So again, this chart can help decide what to focus on to start a transformation—or at least help create a checklist of the practices a team should employ.

49 TRAINING **PRACTICES**

PERCENTAGE OF RESPONDENTS RATING EACH PRACTICE AS CRITICAL

TrainingIndustry.com

95% Listen to uncover real business needs	84% Track course completions & other learning outcomes
95% Use skilled facilitators/presenters	84% Conduct a systematic analysis to develop a plan
94% Use knowledgeable/expert instructors	83% Create easy-to-use support materials
94% Customize training to meet needs	82% Use creativity/innovation in design
93% Establish agreed-upon objectives	79% Schedule instructors, materials & facilities
93% Use industry & job-relevant examples	79% Scale as clients' needs grow
93% Adapt training to business/culture	79% Develop meaningful dashboards/reports
93% Involve experts or thought leaders	75% Use many types of learning technologies
92% Assess/measure learning outcomes	75% Consult to create integration plan
91% Make training engaging & interactive	75% Register learners into courses
91% Collect course feedback from participants	75% Establish areas of expertise
91% Define performance success metrics	74% Collect data using a variety of approaches
89% Assess/measure application/use on the job	73% Leverage experience with other clients
89% Provide training at convenient times	73% Links content to learning technologies
89% Use research-based/reliable info	72% Collect cost data
89% Develop consultative partnerships	71% Interface with corporate-wide systems
88% Add new material & refresh old material	71% Communicate with IT staff
88% Incorporate experiential activities	69% Manage data from multiple sources
88% Assess/measure business outcomes	62% Transition materials to clients
87% Recommend solutions beyond training	61% Manage other vendors/outsource processes
86% Use a variety of methods/tools	55% Track & reimburse tuition expenses
85% Include post-training activities in design	53% Offer a wide range of course topics
85% Offer courses using multiple methods	50% Provide certified/accredited courses
84% Provide training in convenient locations	46% Present courses in different languages
84% Use blended methods for learning	

■ STRATEGIC ALIGNMENT   ■ REPORTING AND ANALYSIS
■ CONTENT DEVELOPMENT   ■ TECHNOLOGY INTEGRATION
■ DELIVERY   ■ ADMINISTRATIVE SERVICES
■ DIAGNOSTIC   ■ PORTFOLIO MANAGEMENT

© 2013 Training Industry, Inc.

Figure 13-3   Forty-Nine Best Practices of Great Training Organizations

The Importance of Leadership

The tools just discussed can really help you work toward getting your training organization focused on the practices that are common in great training organizations—but at the heart of the transformation is leadership. For a training organization to be viewed as great—or, more importantly, to be viewed as a valuable function of the business—there must be strong leadership to make sure the right practices are being performed and at a high level. Learning leaders must ensure that everything the training organization does is aligned to the needs of the business. They schedule regular meetings with the senior management of the organization to get the real picture of the critical objectives of the organization. They bring their voice to the table to share ideas and strategies that demonstrate how training can ultimately move the needle on those objectives.

Training management has evolved from being an academically oriented corporate university—made up of many training courses based on what employees like or dislike, or what they believe is important in helping them to develop their career—to a lean organization focused on mission-critical training that has a direct impact on the overall performance of the business. The benefit is ultimately to the individuals within the business because they are the ones who make an organization successful.

Training leaders are responsible for understanding what training is needed, in partnership with their clients, based on the clients' needs. Training leaders can, and should, have a huge impact on the success of a business, in addition to the success of a training organization.

Measurement

One of the most important strategies in being a great training organization is understanding what the business needs, building an environment of processes and practices that allow you to meet those needs, and continuously measuring your progress so you can adjust and change as requirements shift.

Measurement is about understanding what we currently know and how much we need to know. Those who understand this concept and create systems and practices to make sure they know that their employees know what they need to know—or that their customers know what they need to know—will separate their organizations from being tactical training organizations to being viewed as highly strategic.

The fastest way to success is to develop a plan and systematically stay the course to achieve the desired results. Training is an important means to improving the performance of a business, and having a measurement strategy is critical to systematically making sure that improvements are made on those processes that need to be improved. Improvement is successful only when it is in areas where the business needs it the most.

High-performing training organizations do not just measure activities and outcomes; they systematically measure what is important to measure related to how the processes are performing. They focus their efforts on things that get the business the most return.

The Role of Technology in Learning

The role of technology in learning has evolved from focusing on cost savings to now focusing more on effectiveness. Effectiveness is achieved when learners have the proper level of access to information, to other learners, and to relevant content, with the expectation that it will translate into faster transformation of behavior.

This book examines the four technology platform categories—administrative, delivery, authoring, and collaboration—and considers why their integration is important.

This book also explores the emerging practices of repository management and content curation, a leap into technology-based training, which opens a wide array of data, information, videos, lectures, and discussion groups to the learner. This on-demand, always-on access to training requires a learning leader to formalize the informal world of unmandated content (i.e., search engine) to the kind of organization-specific information that it can mandate and curate and make available through proprietary and protected repositories. These repositories, also referred to as knowledge repositories, are online databases that systematically capture, organize, and categorize knowledge-based information into an easy-to-use and easy-to-access format.

This book also considers how technologies enable learning but can also distract users from learning. And it considers how technology can help drive goals such as consistency for global programs, and how it can solve time and location issues.

Great training organizations that effectively use technology focus on enhancing how a learner consumes content and interfaces with administrators, facilitators, and other learners. Technology should not be cumbersome, difficult to navigate, or intermittent in performance. If it is, it has the potential to be a distraction and get in the way of the learning experience.

One Final Thought

To build a great training organization, leaders of such an organization should focus on the needs of the business first and then make sure the programs they design, build, and deliver those needs. A leader should become a student of the company's objectives, stay current on how those goals are changing, and challenge the relevance of the organization's programs and services.

Learning leaders should create a culture where excellence is an expectation, not an objective. Doing so requires a focus on how to manage training—not on the kind of training to do. The types of training and topics delivered in training will never stop changing because the needs of the business continue to change. Great training organizations are process oriented and do what they need to do to make their clients great!

A

The Research—2008 through 2013

Introduction

For the past six years, Training Industry, Inc., has surveyed learning leaders from a variety of industries to identify the process capabilities and practices that define a great training organization. In 2008, 462 respondents contributed their insight. Another 364 participated in the 2009 study. In 2010, 183 learning leaders contributed to the study, with an additional 221 and 192 taking part in 2011 and 2012, respectively. Finally, in 2013, 187 learning leaders responded to the survey. In total, 1,474 unique respondents from 1,327 organizations contributed their valuable opinions, identifying not only the most critical process capabilities but also the practices within each that propel training organizations from good to *great*. Learning leaders then rated how well their own training organizations perform each process capability to confirm which processes are truly critical and to pinpoint potential areas for improvement.

Key Findings

By evaluating the input of surveyed learning leaders, this report provides a number of insights about great training organizations, including:

- 59% of learning leaders considered strategic alignment to be the *most critical* process capability for great training organizations.
- More than 40% of learning leaders rated strategic alignment, content development, delivery, diagnostics, and reporting and analysis as *critical* process capabilities for great training organizations.
- The practices that learning leaders identified as most critical for each process capability highlighted the importance of customization, expertise, communication, and assessment methods.
- Approximately 26% of learning leaders rated their own training organization as either *good* or *great* in each of the top five process capabilities (i.e., strategic alignment, content development, delivery, reporting and analysis, and diagnostics).

Process Capabilities

Learning leaders were asked to rate the importance of great training companies possessing each process capability. For the purpose of this study, each of the process capabilities is defined below:

- **Strategic alignment**—Ability to design learning programs that align with business objectives.

- **Content development**—Assessment, design, management, and maintenance of content.

- **Delivery**—Ability to manage an instructor network and deliver training using multiple modalities.

- **Diagnostics**—Ability to identify causes of problems and make recommendations.

- **Reporting and analysis**—Ability to define business metrics and report data to make improvements.

- **Technology integration**—Ability to integrate learning technologies with other learning technologies or other corporate applications.

- **Administrative services**—Ability to manage scheduling, registration, technology, and other support functions.

- **Portfolio management**—Ability to manage, rationalize, and maintain large portfolios of programs.

Almost all learning leaders (i.e., 96% or more) rated each of the eight process capabilities as *somewhat important*, *important*, or *critical*; the percentage of learning leaders rating each process capability as *critical* for exceptional training organizations varied considerably (see Figure A-1).

As you can see, learning leaders most frequently endorsed strategic alignment as critical for training organizations. Further, when learning leaders were asked to specify the process capability that was *most critical* for a great training organization to possess, an overwhelming 59% reiterated the importance of strategic alignment (see Figure A-2).

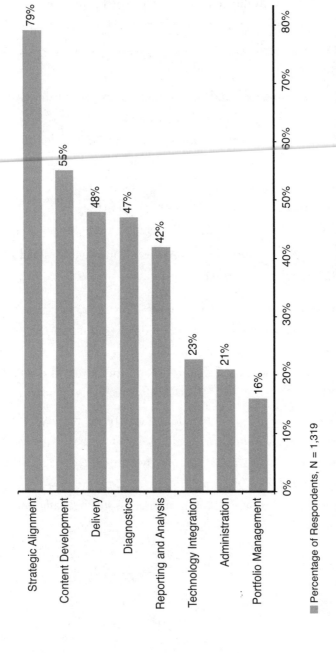

■ Percentage of Respondents, N = 1,319

Figure A-1 Percentage of Respondents Rating Each Process Capability as Critical for a Great Training Organization

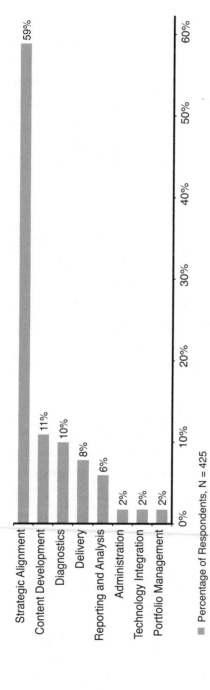

Figure A-2   The Most Critical Process Capabilities for a Great Training Organization

Organization Process Capability Ratings

In all years except 2008, learning leaders were also asked to rate their own training organizations' proficiency in each process capability. The answer choices were don't do/NA, poor, average, good, and great. Figure A-3 shows the percentage of respondents who rated their own training organization as great at each process capability.

A comparison of Figures A-1 and A-3 reveals similar rank ordering of process capabilities. Learning leaders reported that their own training organizations most often excel at four of the top five process capabilities deemed critical to great training organizations: strategic alignment, delivery, content development, and diagnostics.

While 27% of learning leaders rated their training organization as good or great in each of the top five process capabilities (i.e., strategic alignment, content development, delivery, reporting and analysis, and diagnostics), 73% of learning leaders indicated that their training organization was average, poor, or did not do one or more of the top five process capabilities.

Most Critical Practices

In addition to identifying the most critical process capabilities, learning leaders were also asked to rate the importance of several practices for supporting each capability. The top two practices deemed most critical for optimal performance in each process capability are listed below. Not surprisingly, the practices learning leaders identified focus on the importance of customization, communication, expertise, and assessment methods (see Figure A-4).

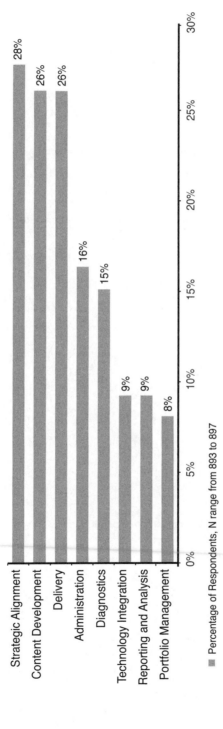

Percentage of Respondents, N range from 893 to 897

Figure A-3   Respondents Rating Their Training Organization as Great for Each Process Capability

Strategic alignment:

1. Customize training to meet the organization's needs.

2. Establish agreed-upon business objectives.

Content development:

1. Use industry, company, or job-relevant examples.

2. Involve subject matter experts or thought leaders.

Diagnostics:

1. Listen to uncover real business problems and needs.

2. Be able to recommend a variety of solutions beyond training.

Delivery:

1. Use instructors with great facilitation and presentation skills.

2. Use knowledgeable or expert instructors.

Reporting and analysis:

1. Assess or measure learning outcomes.

2. Collect course feedback from learners, managers, instructors, etc.

Administrative services:

1. Track course completions, test results, or other learning outcomes.

2. Schedule instructors, course materials, and facilities.

Portfolio management:

1. Use a variety of methods or tools (e.g., online, in person, blended).

2. Add new material and refresh older material.

Technology integration:

1. Be able to use different types of learning technologies (e.g., administrative, authoring, delivery).

2. Use consultative skills to develop an integration plan.

Figure A-4   Top Two Practices for Each Process Capability

Conclusion

Strategic alignment (e.g., aligning training programs with business needs and company goals) was considered the most crucial process capability for training organizations to master, with 79% of learning leaders indicating that it is critical for a great training organization and 59% of learning leaders specifying it as the most critical process capability. In addition, content development, delivery, reporting and analysis, and diagnostics were identified as critical process capabilities. When asked about their own organizations' performance, only 26% of learning leaders rated their training organization as good or great in each of the top five process capabilities (i.e., strategic alignment, content development, delivery, reporting and analysis, and diagnostics). In contrast, 73% of learning leaders indicated that their training organization was average, poor, or did not do one or more of the top five process capabilities, demonstrating room for improvement within the majority of training organizations.

Focusing on the practices that learning leaders identified as most critical within each of these process capabilities provides recommendations that training organizations can use to improve performance. Learning leaders indicated that great training organizations listen carefully in order to identify their clients' business needs. They are responsive to those needs, offering a variety of training delivery methods, tools, technology, and assessment methods. They adapt to best address organizational priorities by creating customized training plans and content. Further, they utilize effective instructors and assess learning outcomes.

Demographics

Approximately 54% of survey respondents were from companies with 500 employees or more (see Figure A-5).

Respondents represented more than 20 industries. The top three industries represented were training and development, technology, and banking/finance (see Figure A-6).

About Training Industry, Inc.

Training Industry, Inc., spotlights the latest news, articles, case studies, and best practices in the training industry. Our focus is on helping dedicated business and training professionals get the information, insight, and tools needed to more effectively manage the business of learning.

For more information, go to www.trainingindustry.com or call 866-298-4203.

About This Research

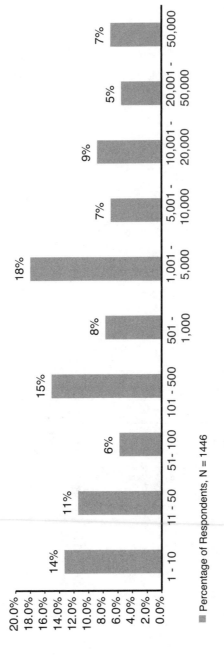

Figure A-5   Company Size (Number of Employees)

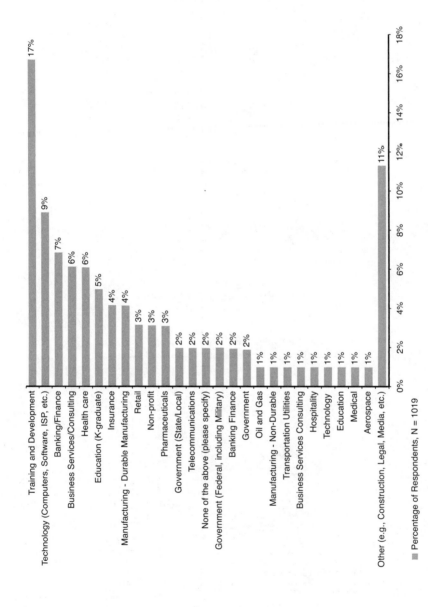

Figure A-6 Industries Represented

Index